WITHDRAWN

Goose and Tomtom

Goose and Tomtom

A Play by DAVID RABE

GROVE PRESS/New York

Published by Grove Press, Inc.
920 Broadway
New York, N.Y. 10010

Library of Congress Cataloging-in-Publication Data

Rabe, David.
  Goose and Tomtom.

  I. Title.
PS3568.A23G6 1987   812'.54   86-29432
ISBN 0-394-56069-8
ISBN 0-394-62351-7 (pbk.)

Manufactured in the United States of America
First Edition 1987

10 9 8 7 6 5 4 3 2 1

For JASON and BLUBY

A man weary of trying to understand his life went into the forest to rest and think, and after walking for a while, he sat beneath a tree in the shade. "How quiet," he thought. "This is such a lovely place. It would be so nice to live here. I wish I had a house in this place."

Because the man had no idea that the tree under which he had seated himself was the Wishing Tree, he was amazed when a grand and spacious house rose up around him. "What a beautiful house," he thought. "What a perfect house I have. How happy I would be if only I was not alone. I wish I had a wonderful woman to be my companion." The woman who sat beside him was loving and tender and beautiful. The man embraced her, and, loving her, he longed to treat her well. "I wish we had something to eat," he thought. The arrival of servants with food was instantaneous, the food varied and delectable and still steaming.

Yet as the man ate, he began to worry. "When I first came here," he thought, "none of this was here. No house, no woman to love me, no food. What is this place? Is this an evil place? Is there a demon here?" And of course the demon was fierce and horrible, scorched and wild, standing in front of the man, shrieking at him. "Oh, he's going to eat me," thought the man.

And the demon ate him.

—A tale told by Muktananda

Not only is the Universe stranger than we think, it is stranger than we can think.

—Werner Heisenberg

I'd rather be a lamppost in Denver than the mayor of Philadelphia.

—Sonny Liston

CHARACTERS

Tomtom	*Lulu*
Goose	*Bingo*
Lorraine	*Men*

Act One

TIME: This was recently.

PLACE: An apartment in the underworld.

The interior of what appears to be a small apartment. Stage right is a tiny kitchen, with a table, some cabinets. Center stage and stage left is a living room, with a couch, armchair, and hassock, all of cheap construction and design. The floor is partly covered with a rug. In the wall of the living room is a doorway to the bedroom, covered by curtains. The bedroom doorway must be prominently placed so that all entrances and exits are instantly visible, and someone merely standing in the doorway would have a powerful stage position. Somewhere along the stage left wall, or perhaps in a tiny little cubbyhole downstage at the farthest point of the stage left area, is a desk and chair on wheels. There are maps and notes, maybe a globe. There are crates piled near the desk. There are crates piled in other areas about the stage, wherever there is an empty upstage spot. The wallpaper is tattered, the cracks of the concrete cinder blocks behind the wall and wallpaper showing through in places. The front door is in the kitchen, and there are many locks on it. Perhaps there is a mirror at the desk, some toilet articles and travel cases. In the kitchen is a window, the blind drawn fully down. Suitcases and crates are piled about in the upstage left corner, and in the desk area, if it is separate from the kitchen area. It might be best to have the desk in a corner of the kitchen and the office chair on wheels located at the kitchen table, enabling Tomtom to scoot back and forth between the kitchen table and the desk. Coats and hats hang on a coat tree by the door or on hooks on the wall there.

3

Lights up. Tomtom lies on the couch, sleeping. He twists suddenly, struggles, groans, and yelps, sitting up. He is a large man, in his forties. He pulls a pistol from a shoulder holster and leaps to his feet, looking warily around. He hurries to the bedroom door and, flattening himself against the wall, is about to slip into the bedroom when he hears a position himself behind the door, it opens. In comes Goose, younger, slighter, carrying a newspaper. He looks around, sees no one.

Goose: Hey.

Tomtom: Hey! *(Kicking shut the door, he jams the gun in Goose's face.)* How you? 'At's what I been waitin' for. I been onna edge a my chair.

Goose: So I'm here. *(They hug, pat each other down, Tomtom's hug evolving into an arm around Goose's neck, a knuckle on the top of Goose's head.)*

Tomtom: Yeh. 'At's good. It's good. How you doin'? You want some coffee?

Goose: You got some coffee?

Tomtom: I could make some. *(He flicks on the switch of a hot plate on which a teakettle sits.)*

Goose: 'At's what I like about you.

Tomtom: What?

Goose: You know.

Tomtom *(threatening to clip Goose)*: You could tell me.

Goose: I don't wanna.

Tomtom *(threatening to clip Goose)*: 'At's okay.

Goose: 'At's what I like about you.

Tomtom *(patting Goose on the cheek)*: *So how you doin'?* *(Tomtom goes to the mirror for cologne, Binaca, Goose following along.)*

Goose: Hey, terrific. Terrific. I'm doin' terrific. I come by. You're here. I was in the neighborhood. I come up the stairs. The door's open. I don't even knock. It ain't locked. I come in. I'm hopin' maybe I'll come in on you, and you an' Lorraine'll be onna floor fuckin'. I can watch. It ain't goin' on, though. You're just here. So we start talkin'. You're sittin' there. I'm standin' over here. We're talkin'. I feel good. You ask me how I'm doin', I tell you fine. I'm doin' fine. How you doin'?

Tomtom: Hey. You're lookin' at me. How do I look? *(Crossing to sit down in the armchair, he grabs Goose's newspaper.)*

Goose: 'At's what I mean. You got an opinion about dreams? I had this fuckin' dream.

Tomtom: Sure I got an opinion.

Goose: What is it?

Tomtom: You really wanna know?

Goose: I'm askin'.

Tomtom: They're a buncha shit.

Goose: You think so?

Tomtom: It's clear as day.

Goose: A buncha shit.

Tomtom: That's what I said.

Goose: A buncha shit.

Tomtom *(standing up)*: You asked for my opinion.

Goose: How long you had this opinion?

Tomtom *(shoving Goose in the chest so Goose goes flying)*: What else you gonna think? What the hell else you gonna tell me? You gonna tell me somethin' else? I mean, you're layin' there, am I right so far? You're layin' there flat on your back, you got all this stuff like, these things like, goin' on under your hat. What the hell else it gonna be, you see what I'm sayin'? I mean, Goose, you was sleepin' you had this dream, right? I mean, this was a dream you had you was flat on your ass. I mean, that's the kinda dream we're talkin' about.

Goose: Yeh.

Tomtom: So what else it gonna be?

Goose: But I remember it.

Tomtom: Big deal. I remember a lotta shit. But it don't mean a fuckin' thing. This green fuckin' witch, she come into my house. I was little. Scared the crap outa me.

Goose: Whatta you talkin' about?

Tomtom: This green goddamn witch. You never heard a such a thing? *(Silence.)*

Goose: Yeh, sure.

Tomtom: You have, huh? *(He hits Goose on one side of the head with the newspaper.)*

Goose: Yeh. Sure.

Tomtom: When? *(He hits Goose on the other side of the head with the newspaper.)*

Goose: Whatta you askin' me?

Tomtom *(gesturing at Goose, who flinches)*: Whatta you sayin' to me?

Goose: You heard me.

Tomtom *(hitting Goose on the side of the head)*: What'sa matter you don't know what I asked you?

Goose: Yeh, I know. I heard you.

Tomtom *(clipping Goose again)*: So whatta we talkin' about?

Goose: I got a headache. You got a headache?

Tomtom: So can I tell my fuckin' story?

Goose: Where's the coffee? You says there was coffee.

Tomtom: What are you, a wise guy? Don't be a wise guy, Goose!

Goose: I want some coffee, I got a headache, you oughta offer some aspirin. I hate aspirin, but I got a headache. *(He clutches his head.)* Oh, oh, oh. It's like a clangor in it, bangin' in this bell. And you're callin' me an asshole. It's all upsettin'. I'm gonna take a nap. I'm gonna lay down. Take a nap. *(He flops down on the floor.)*

Tomtom: I got excited.

Goose: You hurt my feelings.

Tomtom: I got excited.

Goose: You don't have a headache, huh? *(Tomtom takes a bottle of aspirin from some downstage crates and tosses the bottle to Goose.)*

Tomtom *(crossing to the coffee to prepare two cups)*: No. So can I tell my story?

Goose: It's okay. I apologize. You was sayin'?

Tomtom: So this green goddamn witch come into my house. I was little. I could walk, I wasn't crawlin', but I fell over a lot. That was the age I was: where you fall over a lot. And so into this room I was in comes this green goddamn witch with eyes like full of little beehive holes and she's got this snake in her hand; it's wigglin', hissin' like a witch's voice—you want cream?—and she stood lookin' at me. I was playin'; her face was green, her lips had these wrinkles like grooves. She was starin' at me. I fell over backwards. She scared the crap outta me and I fell over backwards. *(He sets the two cups of coffee on the kitchen table.)*

Goose *(moving to join Tomtom)*: A witch, huh?

Tomtom: Yeh.

Goose: I saw a witch once. She wasn't green. She put me in a sack. She tied the top. I was in there. She screamed at me. Her hair was like oil. I was in this sack. Then she dropped me in a buncha water. I was gonna drown. I couldn't get outa the sack. The water was comin' in. Then she took me out and I was almost dead. She was lookin' into my eyes, and she says to me, "You are almost dead." I says, "I am, yes. You're right."

(Tomtom stares, thinking. They sit.)

Goose *(looking around)*: We're just sittin' here.

Tomtom: I'm not.

Goose: Sure you are.

Tomtom: Naw. The sun come out this mornin' an' I saw it. *(Startled; he is just remembering what he saw.)*

Goose: I didn't see it.

Tomtom: I saw it comin'. The clouds were like funnels, all furry, and I could see like specks of phosphorous and hydrogen. These swirls of like blood and these clouds stretchin' out over this flat blue land, a hard dirt, like it was glass it was so hard, and the dawn was comin', I could see it, and this light ran the length of the blue hard dirt before the sun was there—I didn't know what it was. "What's that?" I says.

Goose: I didn't see it.

(Tomtom runs to the door as if to look for what he saw. He looks out the door, out the window.)

Tomtom: I'm tellin' you. It's the sun. And then it was big and red as a wheel of blood slippin' up outa the earth to light down this tunnel I was standin' in, these chambers of cloud, and that was the sunrise. "It's mornin'," I says. *(He slams the door shut and locks it, using all the locks.)*

Goose: And it was?

Tomtom: It was amazin'.

Goose: I wish I'd seen it.

Tomtom *(peeping out the eyehole, as if to make certain nothing is there)*: But I tole you; I tole you. 'At's my point.

Goose: I was sleepin'.

Tomtom: I'm glad you're my friend, Goose.

Goose: I'm glad you're my friend, Tomtom.

Tomtom: You got your gun?

Goose: Oh, yeh.

Tomtom (*pulling out a huge long-barreled pistol from his shoulder holster*): I got my gun.

Goose: I got my gun. (*He pulls out a glistening pistol from his jacket pocket.*)

Tomtom: Look at 'em. Look at 'em . . . guns.

Goose: Bang, bang.

Tomtom: Bang, bang.

Goose: Tell me about the sunrise again, Tomtom.

Tomtom: You wanna go shoot somebody? We could go shoot somebody.

Goose: You wanna?

Tomtom: Who you wanna shoot?

Goose (*looking around the room as if to find somebody there*): You wanna?

Tomtom: We could find somebody.

Goose: Sure.

Tomtom (*playing with his gun as if Goose might be the person to be shot*): Sure. There's lotsa people.

Goose: You know what I would like to do? I would like to find out what fuckin' Bingo's up to.

Tomtom: That bastard.

Goose: He's a turd. Nobody's arguing that fact. But what's he up to?

Tomtom: He's up to somethin', huh?

Goose: I saw him.

Tomtom: I used to love that guy.

Goose: Me too. Who didn't? He was a beautiful guy. I loved that guy, and then he went an' did what he did—havin' Fuckin' Eddie iced.

Tomtom: He was the one who did it.

Goose: Absolutely. He didn't pull the trigger, but he put the money in the handa the muscle that squeezed the fuckin' trigger.

Tomtom: For no reason.

Goose: There was a reason.

Tomtom: No reason.

Goose: There was a reason.

Tomtom: I know Eddie was bangin' Bingo's sister, but that is no reason to burn the kid.

Goose: That's not the reason.

Tomtom: So what was the reason, for crissake?

Goose: I am not at liberty to say.

Tomtom: You are not at liberty to say. You know the reason but you are not at liberty to say. So what is it? *(He takes out a blackjack.)*

Goose: It's information I have been sworn to secrecy about.

Tomtom *(stalking Goose)*: Goose, I tole you about the sunrise. You wouldn't even know it was daylight, I hadn't tole you how the sun come up. You wouldn't know how the light got here. You wouldn't know if it was day or night. So gimme a break.

Goose: Bingo was fuckin' his sister, too.

Tomtom: Bingo was bangin' his own sister, is what you're sayin', and then Eddie started bangin' Bingo's sister too, and this for Bingo was intolerable, so he had Eddie iced? That is interesting. I thought it was protective, you know what I mean, but it wasn't even business. That is interesting. What other secrets are you not at liberty to say? *(Tomtom has his arm around Goose's head.)*

Goose: Nothin'.

Tomtom: Nothin'. Like hell.

Goose: Nothin'. But I would like to know what Bingo's up to, however.

Tomtom *(rushing off to a pile of crates)*: We could wire his rooms. I got the equipment. We could listen on his phone, steam open his mail.

Goose: You wanna start doin' that?

Tomtom: I'd like to bang his sister; wouldn't you like to make her say "Bingo?"

(Tomtom paces away, as Goose digs into the crate, coming out with headphones, which he puts on.)

Goose: We could keep a list a who's comin' and goin' outa his doorways. Front and back.

Tomtom: We'd figure it out. *(Tomtom has a folder taken from the desk. He has a map of the city.)*

Goose: We could get a line on what he's up to.

Tomtom *(making a note in the folder)*: I can smell it.

Goose: I think he's tryin' to expand on his area influence.

Tomtom: He's got enough.

Goose: I'd like to fuck his sister. We could get her up here, tie her up, put a gag in her goddamn mouth, keep her in the closet.

Tomtom *(grabbing up a map, studying it)*: Monkey Murphy's up to somethin' too.

Goose: He's a fake. He ain't up to nothin'.

Tomtom: I been watchin' him. An' he's up to somethin'. I ain't got a line on it yet, but I will. And Connie the Hook over on Elm Street, he's up to somethin'.

Goose: All these fuckin' guys, man.

Tomtom: Yeh.

(The door opens and Lorraine steps in, putting away her keys. They whirl, ducking, pulling their guns and pointing them at her.)

Lorraine *(walking up to Tomtom, as if to kiss him)*: Hey. So you're here. I was lookin' for you.

Goose: Hey, Lorraine, you look beautiful.

Tomtom: We been talkin'. Did you see the sunrise? *(Pushing her aside, he walks to the door, which she has left open. He locks it up again.)*

Lorraine *(to Goose)*: So how you doin'?

Goose *(bragging)*: Hey, all right. I mean, I come over. I come up the stairs, I'm thinkin' this, I'm thinkin' that, I don't know what I'm doin'. So I knock on the door. Tomtom's here. So we're talkin'. There's this sunrise. He's standin', I'm sittin'. He's sittin', I'm sittin'. You ain't here. He's standin', I'm standin'. We're both sittin'! I got this fuckin' headache. He's yellin' at me. We have some coffee. *(While Goose is speaking, Lorraine moves near Goose, quite flirtatiously removing her jacket, her gloves, her scarf.)* Everybody's up to somethin', we don't know what it is. We're tryin' to figure it. Bingo, Monkey, Connie. Eddie. Who iced him. Dumped him in the river. What it is everybody's up to? Somethin'. All of 'em. It's nervous. We don't know what it is. We got our guns, though. He's got his. I got mine.

(He whips out his gun.)

Goose: We don't give a fuck. You come by. You wanna know how we're doin'. All right. Hey, hey. So I'm tellin' you. You're standin'. there. We got our guns out. Tomtom's got a .38 magnum. I got a .38 special. You're standin' there. You ain't smilin'. I'm talkin' on and on. I'm . . . noddin' my fuckin' head. Up and down. *(He is.)* So how you doin', Lorraine?

Lorraine: So how you, Tomtom?

Tomtom *(crossing away from her and toward Goose)*: Hey, I'm all right. You know what I mean—Goose comes in. I'm here, you know, I had a rough night—I'm restless, Goose comes in, I ain't feelin' good and Goose comes in, I'm tryin' to decide about some coffee, and in comes Goose—I ain't even thinkin' about him—there was this sunrise and it was beautiful—so I'm thinkin' about it and Goose comes in—I'm wonderin' about you—how are you feelin'—in comes Goose—you know, you're out all night, it ain't my business, but I worry. It's a bad fuckin' city. So Goose comes in. He surprises me. So we start talkin'. He's got a headache. We're figurin' Bingo's maybe after us, but we don't know. He's a bastard; he's a bastard. So you come in. You wanna know how I'm doin'. I'm okay. I been better an' I been worse. I'm tellin' you, right? I'm tellin' you. I ain't doin' bad. All right! (*He ends up with his arm around Goose's head.*)

Lorraine: You fuckin' guys. You're a great coupla guys.

Goose: All right.

Tomtom: Hey.

Lorraine: I mean, Sally and Linda and Darlene and Carla, they was all talkin' about you. What a great coupla guys! And Sally says, "Goose is tougher," and Darlene says, "Tomtom is tougher." They get into this argument over you guys. Can you see that? So I figured out a way a figurin' it out, let these poor girls have a REST—you got 'em goin' crazy.

Tomtom: Goose is awful tough.

Goose: You're tough, too, Tomtom.

Tomtom: I ain't no tougher than you, Goose.

Goose: I'm awful tough, too. I know that. I scare myself sometimes.

Tomtom: I scare myself too, Goose. Sometimes, I scare myself awful, how tough I am.

Lorraine: So what I figured, we'd have this contest and see who was the tougher by sticking pins in your arms.

Tomtom (*interested*): Yeh.

Goose: All right.

Tomtom: So we stick some pins in our arms and see who's tougher.

Goose: All right.

Tomtom: That's a good idea, Lorraine. *(This may be the best idea he's ever heard in his life.)*

Goose: Goddamn, Lorraine. Broads, huh, Tomtom?

Tomtom: They got these ideas, Goose. Broads. They got these goddamn ideas.

Lorraine: So I'm gonna stick these pins in your arms, and the one who yells first ain't the tougher.

Tomtom: All right. *(Crossing to the couch, he sits and starts rolling up his sleeves.)*

Goose: Fuckin' broads, man.

Tomtom: The one who yells ain't the tougher.

Goose: How many pins you got there, Lorraine? *(Moving to the couch, he starts rolling up his sleeves.)*

Lorraine: Twenty.

Goose: That's ten apiece. She's gonna put ten fuckin' pins in our arms, Tomtom.

Tomtom *(putting his arm around Goose)*: All right.

Lorraine *(crossing to stand behind them)*: Here we go. *(She sticks a pin into Tomtom's arm.)* One.

Goose: How you doin', Tomtom? Can we talk, Lorraine, or is talkin' yellin'?

Lorraine *(pacing behind them)*: And one for Goose. . . . And two for Tomtom, and two for Goose. . . . And three for Tomtom and three for Goose. Talkin' ain't yellin'. You can talk, as long as you don't talk loud. Three for Goose and three for Tomtom.

Tomtom: You're so beautiful, Lorraine. You're so god-damn beautiful. I love you. I love you.

Lorraine: And four for Goose and four for Tomtom.

Goose: I love you too, Lorraine.

(Goose tries to get away every now and then, but Tomtom holds him.)

Tomtom: I'm happy to be doin' this, 'cause it's you doin' it.

Lorraine: Five for Goose and five for Tomtom. You guys are tough.

Tomtom: We are both tough.

Goose: We are maybe equally tough.

Tomtom *(as she sticks number six into both)*: I am very tough.

Goose: Oh, Christ, I love you, Lorraine. I love you. *(Goose tries to get away.)*

Lorraine: Seven for Tomtom and seven for Goose.

(Goose breaks loose, and Tomtom catches him, drags him back, holds him.)

Goose: This is some fuckin' contest, huh, Tomtom.

Tomtom *(loving it)*: All right.

Goose: All right! So how you doin'?

Tomtom: All right. *(He really loves it.)*

Lorraine: Eight for Goose and eight for Tomtom. Nine for Goose and nine for Tomtom. *(Silence. She stands looking at them.)* Ten for Goose and ten for Tomtom.

(Silence. Released by Tomtom, Goose almost falls over, as Lorraine studies them, awaiting a reaction.)

Goose: I'm gonna go to the bathroom. Okay? *(He staggers off. Lorraine paces to the kitchen table, where she sits, taking from her purse a nail file.)*

Tomtom *(crossing to her menacingly)*: So I was wonderin', Lorraine, last night, I was sleepin', or I was layin' there maybe half awake, or somethin', I don't know what I was doin'—you didn't come in, did you, like in a green mask sorta, and you didn't come in and whisper to me real soft and secret how you loved everybody else more than me— how you loved Connie and Monkey Murphy more'n me, an' how you loved Bingo more'n me, an' your voice real whispery; that didn't happen, did it? You didn't do that, did you, whisperin' you was never gonna love me ever again? *(He ends up rooting through her purse.)*

Lorraine: No.

Tomtom *(grabbing her by the arm)*: Did you?

Lorraine: Last night? No.

Tomtom: Some other night? Ever?

Lorraine: No.

(She pulls away as Goose appears, coming out of the bedroom.)

Goose *(as Lorraine goes storming past him into the bedroom)*: Is the contest over or you gonna get more pins?

Lorraine: You guys are both tough.

Goose: We're very fuckin' tough.

Tomtom: Whatta we gonna do now?

Goose: Whatta you wanna do?

Tomtom: How's your headache? Fuckin' broads, man. Jesus.

Goose: I mean, I thought I was gonna scream. Did you think you was gonna scream?

Tomtom: I thought you was.

Goose: I knew I wasn't gonna scream, but I was maybe gonna throw up.

Tomtom: Fuckin' broads, man—she's gotta stick pins in our arms.

Goose: I mean, she's gotta stick pins in our arms. She's outa her skull, man. I mean, how crazy you gotta be, you come into a room and stick a buncha pins in a couple guys' arms.

Tomtom: You gotta be very crazy.

Goose: More'n that, man.

Tomtom: There's somethin' very unfuckin' natural about broads.

Goose: How you gonna trust 'em? I mean, I ask myself that all the time. All the goddamn time.

Tomtom: I love to bang 'em, man. They got the plumbing, you know what I mean? *(He grabs his crotch to show how he loves to bang 'em.)*

Goose *(grabbing his crotch)*: I love to fuck 'em, too. Who's talkin' about that? I mean, like Bingo's sister, keepin' her in the goddamn closet. Tie her up in there, hang her from the hook, take her out, pump her, man, put her back; she wouldn't know what she was doin', but she'd like it.

Tomtom: She'd love it. *(He leaps to his feet, pulling his gun.)* You got a feelin' anybody watchin' us?

Tomtom: No. You?

Goose: No.

Tomtom: Like who?

Goose: I don't know.

Tomtom *(whacking Goose)*: So what'd you say it for? You makin' me nervous.

Goose: Bingo.

Tomtom: That jerkoff. What about him?

Goose: He could be watchin' us. Watchin' us could be part of what he's up to.

Tomtom: Bingo? No way!

Goose: Says who?!

Tomtom: He don't even know where we are.

Goose: I mean, I think we gotta watch him. I mean, he could be watchin' our every move; he could be recordin' our every goddamn word—I mean, like that goddamn conversation we had before, he coulda heard it all. I mean, I don't feel so good. How you think things are goin'?

Tomtom: All right.

Goose: All right. So we got pins in our arms, so what. *(He is sweating, nervous, a little sick.)*

Tomtom: What conversation? *(He's very suspicious.)*

Goose: Before. We was talkin'. We was worried.

Tomtom: Yeh.

Goose: You remember. You think we could take the pins outa our arms or would she get pissed off?

Tomtom: She'd get pissed.

Goose: Sure. I know.

Tomtom: She's a broad, you know what I mean.

Goose: The best, though.

Tomtom: The best. You better believe it.

Goose: The best goddamn broad in town.

Tomtom: You think I'm arguin'? Do I sound like I'm arguin'?

Goose: She's a fuckin' queen, is what she is! So is there anything to drink around here?

Tomtom (*perhaps pulling out a bottle from a hiding place in the couch*): You want some Scotch?

Goose: How about some bourbon?

Tomtom (*heading for the kitchen*): Have us a little pop.

Goose: So, Tomtom, you know what I mean? It don't really matter if Bingo's after us—is that what you're sayin'? We can handle it.

Tomtom: You sayin' we can't? (*Tomtom is setting them up at the kitchen table.*)

Goose: Gimme a double. So if I was to say what I'm wonderin'—and I ain't said it yet—but if I was to say it, you got any idea what you would think a me?

Tomtom: What?

Goose: I got this thing I ain't said it yet.

Tomtom: I know you ain't said it yet.

Goose: I mean, you gonna be mad at me or not?

Tomtom: Fuck no.

Goose: You're mad already.

Tomtom: Goose, have another drink.

Goose: It's okay.

Tomtom: You're such a secretive fuck! *(He pours his bourbon in Goose's crotch and shoves Goose back into the armchair.)*

Goose: Yeh, well, it's embarrassin' to have been a frog.

Tomtom: No it ain't.

Goose: Was you ever a frog?

Tomtom: What?

Goose: I mean, sometimes I still got like these frog feelings from when I was briefly a frog.

Tomtom: Hey, so you think you can't talk to me about that?

Goose: I was wonderin'.

Tomtom: So you were a frog. So what? Am I your friend or not?

Goose: 'At's what I would say.

Tomtom: You think I don't know about stuff like that? I been around, man. Who you think you're talkin' to?

Goose: Tomtom.

Tomtom: And you're Goose.

Goose: You're tellin' me.

Tomtom: Right.

Goose: I know that.

Tomtom: Aw right. So when was this?

Goose: You're awful interested. So maybe I don't wanna talk about it.

Tomtom: Am I makin' you nervous?

Goose: No.

Tomtom: You look nervous.

Goose: No. It's just my expression sometimes I got it on my face. It don't mean nothin'.

Tomtom: You're sayin' the expression on your face don't mean nothin'? *(He moves near Goose and looks into Goose's face.)*

Goose: Naw. Nothin'. it's just there sometimes. You know. It's just there. These expressions, I don't know about 'em. I don't even think about 'em. They're just there, you know.

Tomtom *(still staring into Goose's face)*: I'm feelin' a little nauseous.

Goose: Whatsamatter?

Tomtom: I'm feelin' a little sick to my stomach. I should lay down.

Goose: You can lay down. Maybe you'll feel a little better.

Tomtom: It ain't nothin', though. It's just very sudden.

I'm standin' there talkin'. We're just talkin', it comes over me. *(He lies down on the couch.)*

Goose *(worried, moving behind the couch near Tomtom to examine him)*: Maybe you got one a these influenza bugs. They're around.

Tomtom: Maybe.

Goose: They sneak in you up your nose. They get in there. They start livin' there. They ain't invisible, but you can't see 'em.

Tomtom: So maybe I'll just lay real quiet.

Goose: You can rest.

Tomtom: Yeh.

Goose *(worried, looking around)*: So what am I gonna do?

Tomtom: It's okay.

Goose *(hurrying to the armchair by the couch)*: So I'll just sit over here on this chair. That's what I'll do. An' I'll put my hands on my lap. An' cross' my legs. No. No, I won't cross my legs. It's you an' me, Tomtom. I'm sittin' up an' you're restin'.

Tomtom *(sitting bolt upright)*: So how come I can't see 'em? *(He leaps up, whipping out his gun.)* What? The bugs sneakin' up my nose. How come?

Goose: They're little tiny.

Tomtom: Oh. *(Pause.)* 'At's scary. *(He collapses back down onto the couch.)*

Goose: I'm sittin' here, and I don't look alert, but I got my hand on the butt a my pistol, my toes is tensed, I could leap in a second was somebody to come in that door, and I would be on my knees so they would be shootin' high and missin' me an' I could blow a hole in their belly the size of a sewer, their guts droppin' out like drowned rats.

Tomtom: How come they'd be comin' in here, Goose?

Goose: To get us. *(He runs around now, making defense preparations, barricading the door, looking out the eye-hole, practicing his maneuvers, turning over the armchair to form an* L*-shaped fortification with the couch.)*

Tomtom: How come they'd wanna get us, Goose?

Goose: They'd have their reasons.

Tomtom: Like what, Goose?

Goose: I don't know. They'd know the reasons, though. I mean, Tomtom, there are people out there got reasons to get us.

Tomtom: Oh, yeh.

Goose: You know that.

Tomtom: Sure. I was just wonderin' what they are.

Goose: What?

Tomtom: The reasons. I mean, maybe before you shot 'em, you could ask 'em.

Goose *(hurrying to hide behind the toppled chair)*: I wouldn't have time.

Tomtom: As they were comin' in the door, you could ask real quick, "How come you wanna get us?"

Goose: There wouldn't be time, Tomtom. You know that.

Tomtom: Yeh.

Goose (*patting Tomtom*): So how's your stomach?

Tomtom: You wanna talk about the sunrise again?

(*Goose flops down on the floor behind the toppled arm-chair, and Tomtom leans against the front of the couch, so they seem almost two men in a foxhole.*)

Goose: So how you feel?

Tomtom: These fuckin' pins are killin' me.

Goose: I mean, it was before I lived around here. I don't know where it was, but I was in this room, and I couldn't get out. But I don't give a fuck. It's happened before. And then, all of a sudden, there's all this dark behind me that's different than all the other dark, and in this different dark, there is the reason that it's different, and the reason is it's a ghost behind me, and when I turn to look he just moves so he stays behind me, and then he says like into the back of my head, "Don't you wanna know the secret?" And I say, "No, I don't." An' he says, "It's a secret about you, don't you wanna know it?" And I say, "No," an' I'm wishin' he would go away, and he hears my thinkin', so he's angry.

(*Tomtom spasms, getting sicker, and Goose goes to the downstage crates from which Tomtom got the aspirins. Goose gets a thermometer, a stethoscope, aspirin, perhaps something for the pins. Going back to Tomtom, he tends him.*)

Goose: All of a sudden in his anger I can't move anymore, and then I can, but I can't stand up, or talk. And all of a sudden I know why all the other little kids in the neighborhood hate me, 'cause they do, and tease me, 'cause they do, and it's 'cause I'm a frog. 'At's the secret about me. And now he's brought it up outa the secret places in me and into my body; this ghost with these eyes has looked at me an' turned me into a frog in me. *(Pause.)* Well, I'm cryin'—I'm not afraid to tell you, Tomtom, I'm cryin' an' beggin', I'll do anything he wants—I don't know what it is—but I can't move or speak, all green and spotty. So the night is on and on, and it's truer than anything else. I belong on my belly. Out of doors an' wet and cold. Out by green scummy ponds unable to talk all my feelin's or thoughts but burstin' with 'em. Layin' inna wet slimy grass, hopin' to lick some fly outa the air. Worms around me an' spiders. The night seems so long. As years an' years. And then there's light, an' I see my body's a person again, 'cause I made the ghost a promise I don't know what it was. *(Slight pause.)* An' sometimes, I still get feelings of a frog an' I gotta look around and check everything real good an' make sure I'm not layin' in green wet grass wantin' to eat flies, 'cause I'm cold in my heart sometimes. I'm all spotty an' green in my heart. In my heart I know where I belong, an' I got big buggy eyes. *(Pause.)* That fuckin' promise to a ghost, I made it—I don't know what it was, but I know I'm keepin' it. He said I would be a frog as long as he was a ghost, and blood was red and mud wet an' secrets secrets. You ever made a promise to a ghost? Tom . . . tom?

(The lights have dimmed to evening.)

Tomtom: No.

Goose: You're lucky.

Tomtom: Last night. I was surrounded by 'em. It was awful.

Goose: 'At's what I'm sayin'. An' you didn't make any promises to 'em?

Tomtom: I wish I was a happy person.

Goose: I wish I was a happy person too, Tomtom. I wish we both was. You wish we both was? Or just you was.

Tomtom: I wish we both was.

Goose: Me too.

Tomtom: It would make me too unhappy if you was unhappy.

Goose: Me too. You happy or unhappy right now?

Tomtom: Unhappy. Unhappy.

Goose: Me too.

Tomtom: I mean, Bingo's got everything goin' for him an' everybody's up to somethin'. I got ghosts in here at night. Lorraine's gone. You know what I mean? Out on the streets. She's out there. Doin' what? I don't know. Who knows? You know? It scares me how she's out there on the street. I'm up all night. How'm I gonna be happy? You see what I'm sayin'?

Goose: Sure.

Tomtom: How about you?

Goose: I ain't happy.

Tomtom: You ain't happy.

Goose: I wish I was happy.

Tomtom: I wish you was, too.

Goose: I don't know.

Tomtom: You cryin'? *(He reaches suddenly to turn on a lamp.)*

Goose: Yeh.

Tomtom: How come?

Goose: I don't know.

Tomtom: You wanna put on your cowboy suit? We could put on our cowboy suits.

Goose: Naw.

Tomtom: We both could put on our cowboy suits.

Goose: I don't wanna.

Tomtom: How about your hat? Put on your hat. *(He hurries to the upstage crates to get the hat.)*

Goose: Naw.

Tomtom: C'mon.

Goose: Naw.

Tomtom: C'mon, Goose. You'll feel better. Just the hat.

Goose: It's a great fuckin' hat. *(Tomtom puts the hat on Goose: a Stetson.)*

Tomtom: All right!

Goose: How do I look?

Tomtom: Fantastic.

Goose: I bet I do.

Tomtom: I wish you was here an' that hat on when them ghosts come by last night. I mean—they ask me how I'm doin'? So I tell 'em. Lorraine's out on the street. I can't sleep. I'm up all night. Now they're here lookin' at me outa these little holes in the hoods they are wearin', which are black an' their eyes scary. They're psychos, you know. Psycho ghosts with evil hearts under their sheets wavin' in the wind comin' in the window 'cause I left it open in the hope Lorraine passin' by on the street below, she might call to me or I might sniff her perfume, I could call to her. How they think I'm doin'? I got ghosts come into my room with evil in their hearts and they glow like the moon standin' at the foot of my bed. Then they tie me down with invisible ropes, explainin' how they have come for somethin' and they don't know where it is, but they will look for it and find it and they can only look for it and find it if I got this blindfold over my eyes, so they put it over me and I hear 'em moving things which they are picking up and putting down, and one of them says he sympathizes with my predicament, but the only way to do the things they are doing is the way they are doing them. He leans near to me, whispers, and his breath has a stink in it and I cannot follow the line of his lingo, and I try to melt the cold growing in me, and the melting cold comes out of my body in sweat and from my eyes in tears, and they are moving things still, picking things up and putting things down. And I'll never guess who they are, the one who sympathizes with my predicament says, or what they're looking for, but when they find it—and they will—they'll take it and be gone. All this was last night.

(Tomtom has been breaking out crates of weapons, putting the chair back in place and putting on additional shoulder holsters, along with knives and pistols strapped to his ankles. He has hidden weapons in the couch. He has made a Molotov cocktail and hidden it in a drawer. Goose has watched intently all the while.)

Goose: Did you promise 'em nothin'?

Tomtom *(checking the peephole in the front door):* Nothin'.

Goose: And they left.

Tomtom: I didn't see 'em, and I don't know what they took. *(He grabs a map.)*

Goose: Where was I?

Tomtom: You wasn't here.

Goose: So I come by this morning. I'm here, we're talkin'.

Tomtom: After the sunrise; you didn't see it. You come by. Lorraine comes by. The pins. Lorraine—

Goose *(grabbing one of the hidden weapons to arm himself further):* The fuckin' pins. YOU THINK I'M GONNA FORGET? NOT THIS BOY! NOT YOUR GOOSE. SO HOW WE DOIN'?

Tomtom: I don't know. *(He takes the weapon from Goose and angrily hides it again.)*

Goose: You don't know how we're doin'?

Tomtom: We're talkin'. *(He grabs half of an old sandwich off the desk.)*

Goose: I got my hat on.

Tomtom: You got your hat on.

Goose: I'm nervous. *(Coming up to Tomtom, he is chased away.)*

Tomtom: I'm hungry. You hungry?

Goose: I'm nervous.

Tomtom: I'm hungry.

Goose: I'm nervous.

Tomtom: You hungry?

Goose: I'm nervous, you're hungry.

Tomtom: Yeh.

Goose: You're hungry.

Tomtom: I'm hungry. You're nervous.

Goose: I am very nervous. I am feelin' very nervous. SO HOW WE DOIN'? *(He rushes up to Tomtom.)*

Tomtom: That fuckin' Bingo!

Goose: That's what I mean. That's what I mean, that fuckin' Bingo; he got everything goin' for him. How come you ain't nervous?

Tomtom *(grabbing Goose by the shirtfront)*: Whatta you askin' me?

Goose: You sayin' you don't know what I'm askin' you?

Tomtom: Would you say from my behavior, I am actin' like I do?

Goose: Am I actin' like you don't?

Tomtom: You want me to tell you you ain't makin' any fuckin' sense, Goose? Is that what you want? Whatta you want?

Goose: Whatta you mean whatta I want?

Tomtom: You sayin' you know what you're sayin'?

Goose: I'm sayin' it ain't unclear to me what I want is what I'm sayin'.

Tomtom: Whatta you sayin' to me?

Goose: Whatta you askin' me, Tomtom? HOW COME YOU AIN'T NERVOUS?

Tomtom: You don't know by now, I could care? You think I care? *(Grabbing the cowboy hat off Goose, he hits Goose with the hat.)*

Goose: No.

Tomtom: Right! *(He shoves Goose and hurls the hat so it lands by the bedroom door.)*

Goose: I'm feelin' very confused. I'm feelin' very confused. I feel like hoppin' a little. I'm gonna just be hoppin' a little.

Tomtom: That's good; that's good. You done a little boxin', no doubt. *(From the crates by his desk, Tomtom is breaking out target figures, one of which is full size; several others may be half size.)*

Goose *(following Tomtom around as he puts up a target with a staplegun or at least looks for the places to put them)*: So I'm wonderin', Tomtom, I'm wondering to myself, and I'm gonna maybe include you briefly in my wonderin' by lettin' it out loud, though unimportant, and I wouldn't want you takin' it with no seriousness, but I'm wonderin'—For godsake, we're tryin' to get to the bottom of it all. I'm losin' track what I'm sayin'—what am I sayin'—what am I sayin'—did you look into her eyes? She was right down next to me, I'm wonderin' did you look into her eyes?

Tomtom: Whatta you mean?

Goose: Did you look into her eyes?

Tomtom: I don't know what you mean.

Goose: I'm sayin' did you look into the eyes a Lorraine, she was puttin' the pins. I couldn't look into her eyes! I don't know why I couldn't except I might disappear.

Tomtom: You're sayin' you thought if you looked into her eyes, you might disappear, and you're askin' me did I look into her eyes? DO I LOOK CRAZY?

Goose: Why would it be crazy?

Tomtom: You wanna fuckin' disappear? You look into her eyes, you'll fuckin' disappear! Listen to me—

Goose: —I'm still hoppin', I'm still hoppin'—

Tomtom: —Listen to me: you trust me, right? Am I right so far?

Goose: Right.

Tomtom: So how come I gotta tell you what you already know? And you don't talk about it ever again, either. You don't talk about it. Don't you know she can hear you?

Goose: Whatta ya mean?

Tomtom: She can hear your every word.

Goose: Who? Lorraine?

Tomtom: Always! Always!

Goose: She's in the other room!

Tomtom (*furious*): I can't stand these pins anymore, I can't stand 'em!

Goose: Ahhhhhhhhhhhhhhhhhgggggggggggggggghhhhhh!

Tomtom: No. Goose, don't; not so loud.

Goose: Ahhhhhhhhhhhhhhhhhgggggggggggggggghhhhhh!

Tomtom: We gotta gut it out; we gotta—

Goose: Ahhhhhhhhhhhhhhhhgggggggggggggghhhhhh! *(They struggle, Tomtom trying to quiet Goose.)*

Tomtom *(enraged)*: Ahhhhhhhhhhhhhhhhggggggggggggggghhhhhh! Ahhhhhhhhgggggggghhhhhh!

Goose *(in pain)*: Ahhhhhhhhhhhhhhhhhgggggggggggggggghhhhhh!

(The struggle carries them onto the couch. Lorraine comes into the room and stands looking at them.)

Tomtom: Ahhhhhhhhhgggggggggghhhhhh!

Goose: Ahhhhhhhhhhgggggggggghhhhhh!

Lorraine: So what's goin' on?

(Instantly, they take up casual poses on the couch.)

Tomtom: Nothin'.

Goose: Nothin'.

Lorraine: I thought maybe the pins was hurtin'.

Goose: Nawwwww.

Tomtom: Nawwwww.

Goose: You hurtin', Tomtom?

Tomtom: Nawwwww.

Goose: Some contest, Lorraine. Never a dull moment with broads, man.

Lorraine: So we got trouble an' I come out to tell you. You like this dress?

Tomtom: It's real nice, is my opinion. You got an opinion, Goose?

Goose: It's real nice. So what's the trouble?

Tomtom: It's a beautiful dress. So what's the trouble? I don't see no trouble.

Lorraine: Do you see what I am not wearing?

Tomtom: I think you look real attractive, Lorraine.

Lorraine: But what am I *not* wearing?

Tomtom: I don't know.

Goose: You are not wearing a *truck,* Lorraine! You are not wearing a *tree,* Lorraine.

(Tomtom whacks Goose on the back of the head.)

Lorraine: What else am I not wearing, Tomtom?

Tomtom: You look so beautiful, it doesn't matter.

Lorraine *(suddenly in a state of high emotion)*: I am not wearing any jewels. I have no jewels!

Tomtom: What?

Lorraine: Our jewels. Our gems from all our heists. I was going to wear them—I was going to come out glittering with jewels—so I went to the closet and—we been ripped off, you know what I mean, we been had—there's nothin' in the closet but this broad hangin' there by her hands, this gag in her mouth, this blindfold on her eyes—all my jewels are gone, my gems, my pearls and diamonds. Somebody has come in here and ripped us off. I thought you was here all the time, Tomtom—didn't I ask you— isn't that what I asked you? *(She berates Tomtom, yelling in his face.)*

Tomtom: I did; I did; I thought I did; I don't know what it is could have happened.

Lorraine: That's what I'm askin'! You are not askin' me! And who's the fucking broad in the closet? I do not like this uncooperative horseshit!

(Tomtom turns and smacks Goose in the head. Then he turns back to Lorraine.)

Tomtom: Bingo's sister.

Lorraine: That's what I thought. That's who I thought it was.

Tomtom: You was right.

Goose: What's goin' on?

Tomtom *(threatening Goose)*: Goose, c'mon, you know.

Goose: Sure I do.

Tomtom *(moving to join Lorraine, who stands behind Goose)*: Goose's got her in there—he likes to take her out, you know, pump her, put her back. You know how it is.

Lorraine: Sure.

Goose: So you don't mind, Lorraine?

Lorraine: Whatta you askin' me?

Goose *(as Tomtom is moving off toward the kitchen)*: I don't know; I don't know what I'm askin' you. Tomtom knows. What am I askin' her?

Tomtom: Goose, c'mon, don't fuck around.

Goose: I'm okay. *(Goose tries to follow Tomtom)*.

Tomtom: So relax.

Goose: I'm relaxed.

Tomtom: So ask Lorraine the question.

(Anger from Tomtom, along with threatening gestures, keeps Goose in the living room with Lorraine, as Tomtom sits down at the kitchen table with a newspaper or map and Lorraine flops down on the couch beside Goose.)

Goose: I don't wanna.

Tomtom: C'mon, for crissake, I ain't got all day.

Goose: So how you doin', Lorraine?

Lorraine: Fine.

Goose: Good. Me too, you know. So I come by, you know. I come by, I had this bad night, so I'm out on the street, I come by and see Tomtom, am I right so far, Tomtom? So we're talkin', and he ain't feelin' good, and I ain't feelin' so good either. We both had better days, you might say.

(Bingo's sister, a beautiful, tall girl, enters, staggering on from the bedroom. She has a gag in her mouth and is blindfolded and bound. She bumps into something, making a loud noise. Goose, Tomtom, and Lorraine all look. Goose bolts to Tomtom.)

Goose: I mean, Tomtom, I thought we was talkin' about we was MAYBE gonna go get Bingo's sister, you know what I mean?

Tomtom: I DON'T REMEMBER! *(Grabbing Goose, he runs him to the couch and hurls him back down beside Lorraine.)*

Goose *(to Lorraine)*: I don't remember. So you know, one thing leads to another, he's over there, I'm over here, he's sittin', I'm standin', I'm layin' down, we're talkin' about Bingo—blagh, blaghhh—we gotta make a plan, make some moves—

(Bingo's sister is on the move again, and Tomtom is up near the sink, where he pulls a bottle and a rag from a drawer.)

Goose *(continuing)*: So . . . we don't know what we're doin', what's goin' on—so I go over, you know, I go out, I make a move, I duck a little, make a play . . . *(Goose goes running to Tomtom.)* Am I right so far, Tomtom?

Tomtom: I DON'T KNOW! *(Shoving Goose aside, Tomtom advances on the girl. The bottle is chloroform, and he is dumping it on the rag as he moves.)*

Goose: You don't know.

Tomtom: WHATTA YOU THINK? I DON'T KNOW!

(The girl has made her way downstage to the area in front of the couch by the time Tomtom grabs her. He puts the rag to her face as she struggles, and Goose, trailing along, sits on the couch because that is his place.)

Goose: So I'm here, we're talkin'. I wanna this, I wanna that. You know what I mean, Lorraine? You know how it goes?

Lorraine: Sure.

Goose: Sure.

Tomtom: Yeh.

Goose: No big deal.

(The girl lies still on the floor before them now as Tomtom stands up.)

Tomtom: You got an opinion on all this, Lorraine?

Lorraine: So you like to take her out and pump her, huh, Goose, and otherwise you keep her in the closet.

Tomtom *(hitting Goose with the rolled-up newspaper)*: If it bothers you, Lorraine, he can stop.

Lorraine: You keep the gag on her or off her when you're pumpin' her?

(Tomtom hits Goose with the newspaper again.)

Goose: Hey. Whatta ya askin' me? On her; you know.

Lorraine: The blindfold?

Goose: On. Hey, you know.

(Tomtom sits down in the armchair to read the newspaper, using it to separate himself from Goose and Lorraine.)

Lorraine: You keep her tied up? Huh? Look at me, Goose.

Goose: No. Hey.

Lorraine: You keep her tied up? You keep the ropes on her wrists?

Goose: Yeh. It's just the way I do it; you know. Whatta I know?

Lorraine: Look at me, Goose; c'mon, look me in the eye.

Goose: I don't wanna.

Lorraine: C'mon. How long you been doin' this with her?

Goose: I don't know. I ain't so sure. I feel like eatin' a worm, Tomtom.

Lorraine: Tell me how long. You know.

Goose: I don't. Do I, Tomtom?

Lorraine: Look into my eyes.

Goose: Wanna hear about the sunrise? Tomtom saw it. He can tell about it so you think you saw it, sorta.

(Tomtom whacks Goose with the newspaper.)

Lorraine: I want to look into your eyes and see you, Little Goose.

Goose: I ain't in there. I ain't in my eyes.

Lorraine: Let me look.

Goose: I ain't been there for a long time; I ain't in the expressions on my face and I ain't in my eyes. I don't know where I am.

Lorraine: Do you love me?

(Tomtom, with the newspaper spread wide in his hands, lifts it, making a wall that hides his face.)

Goose: You know I do. But you're too beautiful for me to look at. Don't make me. Tom . . . tom . . . ! *(She is lifting Goose's face toward her.)*

Tomtom: I ain't lookin'!

Goose: Help me!

Tomtom: I can't; I can't.

Goose *(looking)*: Ohhh, you got eyes. You got eyes, Lorraine. And your nose, so little skin, with little bones, and little holes in your skin. Your mouth, Lorraine, oh, your teeth, Lorraine. (*Like a baby, Goose paws Lorraine's face; he pulls at her cheeks and mouth, finding surprise after surprise.*) Oh, . . . tongue, your tongue.

(*Tomtom, having lowered the newspaper, is staring at Lorraine and Goose. Slowly, as Goose continues to speak, Tomtom stands up.*)

Goose: I'm lookin' into your face. Ohhh, we are all gonna die. (*Goose feels Tomtom's rage behind him and sees in Lorraine's face a cause for his feelings. He clutches her as Tomtom now towers over him.*) We are all gonna die. The dirt is gonna get us sooner than we expect. (*Goose looks up at Tomtom. Goose is very sad. Tomtom pulls a length of newspaper from his pocket.*) I been lookin' in her face, Tomtom. So how'm I doin'?

(*Tomtom whacks Goose with the newspaper. He hurls Goose to the opposite end of the couch and whacks him with the newspaper.*)

Goose: You know what I mean? I'm onna street. I'm walkin'. I come by. Tomtom's worried.

(*To escape, Goose leaps over the back of the couch. Enraged by this, Tomtom begins to pursue Goose, who, fleeing, uses the couch as a barrier between himself and Tomtom.*)

Goose: Tomtom's worried. He's been up all night. He don't know where you are. It's awful, he don't know where you are or where you been. It makes this hurtfulness in his stomach, and it hurted me, too.

(*Bolting from the living room to the kitchen, Goose tries to get the kitchen table between them, as Tomtom comes running after him.*)

Goose: So how'm I doin'? *(Goose gets hit and grabs up a chair from a set of chairs piled in the corner.)* I am Goose!

(Tomtom smacks the table, knocking things off, and Goose raises the chair over his head.)

Goose: I am Goose and this is a chair!

(Tomtom steps in, daring Goose, hitting Goose with the newspaper, and Goose smashes the chair down on Tomtom's head.)

Goose: I am Goose and I can break a chair! *(Tomtom falls, and Goose runs to the living room, dragging the remnants of the chair with him.)* I am Goose, I wanna eat worms. *(He grabs Lorraine, threatening her with the hunk of chair.)* I ain't feelin' so good. Did you see any looks in my eyes like from a watery and eerie creature? Do you know what I'm sayin' to you? WHAT'S THIS? *(He hurls Lorraine aside and runs to Bingo's sister on the floor.)* What's this? *(He tugs at Bingo's sister and pulls the gag from her mouth.)* I am Goose and what's this? What is this? I can do what I want. What should I do? What should I do? *(His hands are on Bingo's sister.)* What should I do?

Lorraine *(hiding)*: What do you want?

Goose: I am Goose!

Lorraine: What do you want to do? *(Perhaps Goose sees Tomtom stir.)*

Goose: Tomtom, where is Goose?

Tomtom *(waking up, sitting up; there is blood on his forehead)*: Hello. Well, where did I go? Well, where did I go?

Goose: Do you see Goose, Tomtom?

Tomtom: I do. He is kneeling by a broken chair.

Goose: Is he happy?

Tomtom: I don't know. It's hard to tell.

Goose: What about the expression on his face?

Tomtom: It's hard to tell.

Goose: Can't you see?

Tomtom: I don't know.

Lorraine: What about my pearls?

Goose: What pearls?

Lorraine: My pearls and gems; my diamonds.

Goose: I don't know where they are.

Lorraine: Someone stole them.

Goose: I don't know who.

Tomtom: We'll get some new ones, Lorraine, a buncha new ones. Don't worry.

Goose: Are you worried, Lorraine? Don't be worried. We'll take care of you; we promise. We'll get 'em back. We'll go on a journey. There'll be oceans and mountains. We'll hack it. We'll cross 'em and swim 'em. Don't worry.

Lorraine: I wanted to dress up in lovely silks with scarves and all our jewels, so you would smile and be happy at the sight of me.

Tomtom: I'm smilin', Lorraine.

Goose: We can do that.

Lorraine: But it's not a happy smile, Tomtom. Those are not happy smiles.

Tomtom: I'll fix it. We'll make up a plan. I'll make up a plan. *(He moves toward her on the couch.)*

Goose: Whatta ya mean?

Tomtom: I'll make up a plan.

Goose: Whatta ya mean?

Tomtom: We got our guns. You got yours.

Goose: Did you hear a noise? *(Whirling as if he has heard a loud noise, he leaps to his feet, gun drawn.)*

Tomtom: What?

Goose: I heard a noise. *(He runs to hide up by the door.)*

Tomtom *(approaching Lorraine on the couch, trying to make up)*: We gotta make a plan! You got your gun, I got mine. Bang, bang. So whatta you say, Lorraine? It's gonna be all right. We'll make a big score. You make a big score, Lorraine, and you go from poor to rich overnight. You go from nothin' to somethin'. I mean, we're here, Lorraine, you see what I'm sayin'. We're here. We lost our gems, so we're like this—like we are—you there, me here, Goose over there, but we make a big score and it's all different, we're all different, whatever we want, we got it.

(Tomtom is on the couch now, and slowly he and Lorraine move into an embrace. She all but curls up on his lap.)

Tomtom: We go in, see—we're wavin' our guns, they fill our hands with money—it's magical—our hands are empty, an' then they're full, an' you want diamonds, we got all the diamonds you want, all the cars and furs. You're happy. You smile at me; you don't go out on the streets anymore. We cuddle; we hug; we sing little songs, makin' 'em up as we go. Where you goin'?

(Lorraine pulls away from his embrace and walks out the bedroom door, leaving Tomtom.)

Tomtom: Where's she goin', Goose? What door is that? She went out that door.

Goose: I saw her.

Tomtom: Where's she goin'? What door is that?

Goose: I don't know.

Tomtom: I don't remember. Where is she?

Goose: I don't know. I could look. You could look.

Tomtom: I don't wanna.

Goose: She's sleepin'.

Tomtom: How do you know?

Goose: I don't.

Tomtom: She could be dead. Or gone out on the street, out a window, or she coulda been stolen, kidnapped, anything. Go look.

Goose: You do it.

Tomtom: Or she could be dyin' right this second, havin' a heart attack.

Goose: A what?

Tomtom: A heart attack, where your heart attacks you.

Goose: Your heart attacks you?

Tomtom: Fuck you!

Goose: Fuck you! *(Goose's gun goes off and they both hit the floor.)*

Tomtom: You heard a noise. You heard a goddamn noise! *(He bandages his head.)*

Goose *(checking in drawers, waste cans, ready to shoot anything he finds)*: A sneakin' noise. You know what I mean, Tomtom, I kept thinkin' we was gonna find out if she was happy or sad, and if she was sad we'd figure out what to do to make her happy—she's happy—she'll take the pins out of our arms; or we make her happy and she takes the pins out of our arms, but she walks outa the room!

(He has ended at the couch, pounding the spot where Lorraine was just sitting. He is having a little fit. Suddenly there is a loud rumble of thunder.)

Tomtom: Ohhhhhhhhhh.

Goose: What?

Tomtom: What? Didn't you hear her?

Goose: Hear her what?

Tomtom: Her anger; her anger.

Goose: I heard the thunder.

Tomtom: What thunder? *(Again, a rumble of thunder.)*

Goose: That thunder.

Tomtom: Who are you sayin' made that noise, Goose? What are you sayin' to me?

Goose: The sky; it made the thunder.

Tomtom: The sky made that angry noise, that awful rumbling angry noise? Is that what you're saying?

Goose: Yeh.

Tomtom: And who is the sky so angry at, huh? Huh? Who is the sky so mad at?

Goose: It's gonna rain.

Tomtom: You're tellin' me that wasn't an angry, awful noise? You who didn't even see the sunrise, you are sayin' that angry awful rumbling noise wasn't an angry awful rumbling noise? Is that what you're doing? Jesus Christ, Goose, next thing I know you'll be telling me you didn't disappear when you looked into her eyes.

Goose: What?

Tomtom: Is that what you're gonna say, Goose? Huh? Is it?

Goose: No.

Tomtom: So whatta you gonna say?

Goose: Nothin'. I ain't sayin' nothin'. Whatta you sayin'?

Tomtom: You didn't hear me?

Goose: I heard you. I heard you, you're sayin' I disappeared.

Tomtom: Are you sayin' you didn't?

Goose: I ain't sayin' nothin'. I ain't sayin' nothin'. I'm movin' my mouth but you're the one talkin'. You're the one sayin' you couldn't see me I was lookin' into Lorraine's face, I disappeared. I ain't sayin' nothin'. I'm just standin' here. That's all I'm doin'. I'm just Goose standin' here. You sayin' you ain't sayin' what I'm sayin'?

(He has ended kneeling on the floor, hiding his head near Bingo's sister, the spot where he was when Tomtom woke up after having been hit on the head by the chair. There is a loud roar of thunder, very close; lightning in the window.)

Tomtom: We gotta make a plan!.

(Tomtom runs to the kitchen table and grabs some pens and a huge pad on which to draw his plan.)

Goose: How long was I gone?

Tomtom: What?

Goose: When I looked into her eyes and you couldn't see me.

Tomtom: We gotta make a plan!

Goose: I bet it was a long, long time. I bet it was a long, long, long time. I coulda been anywhere. I coulda done anything. Where'd I go? What'd I do? I don't know. You don't know. *(Wandering about, looking for himself, looking for where he might have gone, he ends up again on the floor by Bingo's sister.)*

Tomtom: What we gotta do is get money! To go about all over the earth trying to steal some duplicates just like she lost would take forever. We don't have forever. She'd be unhappy forever. So we'll steal money, and with the money we'll go to a store and in the store we'll purchase the gems and jewels. So this is the plan with which we steal the money to buy the jewels and buy the gems to bring back the smile of Lorraine. There's a bank. A bank. A big red bank. Brick-red walls. Full of money. A black safe. A huge hole full of money. So we'll take our guns. We'll take a car. We'll drive the car down a shady street. Past quiet houses. Everybody's busy. Nobody's lookin'.

Goose: Where'm I?

Tomtom: With me.

Goose: I'm in the car with you?

Tomtom: Got it.

Goose: Good. You're drivin'. *(He pulls the hassock up beside Tomtom and sits.)*

Tomtom: So what we'll do is park the car just down the street a little from the bank.

Goose: Just a little is how far?

Tomtom: Twenty yards.

Goose: What's the name of this bank?

Tomtom: I don't know. It's red brick.

Goose: So we got our car parked twenty yards down the street from this red-brick bank, we don't know its name. So . . . we get out. *(Goose rises, steps out of the car.)*

Tomtom: We got our guns.

Goose *(pulling out his gun)*: I got mine.

Tomtom: We're walkin' up the street. No one notices us.

Goose: Who's gonna notice us, 'cause we're dressed up in businessmen's suits. *(From the clothes tree he grabs two hats, putting one on Tomtom, the other on himself.)*

Tomtom: Right.

Goose: We got those little suitcases like very important men in business always got 'em. *(Dashing upstage, he grabs two suitcases, putting one on Tomtom's lap, holding the other himself.)*

Tomtom: Briefcases.

Goose: We got these briefcases.

Tomtom: The bank's full of money.

Goose: We got these briefcases an' the bank's fulla money, and we're walkin' up the street. *(Goose starts to stroll off.)* Nobody knows what we're up to. We got 'em all fooled.

Tomtom: So we come up to this mailbox and at the mailbox we're gonna synchronize our watches.

Goose: So we're doin' that, right, I don't know what it is.

Tomtom: It's we make our watches say the same thing.

Goose: So whatta we make 'em say?

Tomtom: We make 'em say five of three.

Goose: What time is it?

Tomtom: Five of three. Almost closing time.

Goose: Good.

Tomtom: Or do you mean now?

Goose: What?

Tomtom *(hurrying to Goose to straighten things out)*: Now? Do you mean now?

Goose: What?

Tomtom: Wait a minute; wait a minute.

Goose: No, no. After the thing there and the street and we're by the mailbox there, and we do the thing there by the mailbox, you know with our watches—so what happens next?

Tomtom: You mean in the plan?

Goose: Yeh. I mean, fuckin' A. That's what we're talkin' about. The plan!

Tomtom: Well, maybe when we're really doin' it! I thought you was askin' what was gonna happen then when we're really doin' it.

Goose: Oh.

Tomtom: You know.

Goose: Yeh.

Tomtom: I don't know that. That's what I'm sayin'. There's no way to know that, so I hope you're not askin' that. I mean, I know you're not—I just, you know—I mean, I know, you know. That's why we're makin' the plan—that's why we're talkin' about the goddamn plan, we can know what's happenin' in the plan. Right?

Goose: Right.

Tomtom: Okay.

Goose: You know, I'm gettin' depressed.

Tomtom: What'sa matter?

Goose: I'm just thinkin'.

Tomtom: 'At's okay.

Goose: I mean, they probably got us spotted already; we are not as inconspicuous as we would like in our business suits no matter how hard we're tryin' to look unlike ourselves. They got us spotted. We're out there by the mailbox, you know, and we're doin' this stuff about five of three to our watches, and somebody's probably looked out the window and seen us and said there's two crooks out there pretendin' they're businessmen. So the place is crawlin' with cops. That's what I'm thinkin'.

Tomtom: You mean, there's cops comin'.

Goose: Yeh.

Tomtom: We gotta fight 'em. *(Tomtom tries to make the appropriate revision or even a new plan, ripping up sheets.)*

Goose *(pointing to the plan)*: There's too many.

Tomtom *(revising)*: No.

Goose *(hitting the plan)*: There's too many. We gotta run. We take off runnin'. *(He runs.)*

Tomtom: We stand and fight. We got guns that never miss. We got bullets that knock 'em down like steam rollers! *(Ripping a calendar down from the wall, Tomtom jams his plans onto the hook so it hangs there.)*

Goose: I'm in a alley trapped, Tomtom. They got me; they're gonna get me.

Tomtom *(working on his plan on the wall)*: Don't give up.

Goose: They got me. I thought I was tougher.

Tomtom: I don't feel good. I don't feel good.

Goose: I don't feel good.

Tomtom: I feel sick.

Goose: I don't know what's goin' on.

Tomtom: I feel awful. Like I ate some poison.

Goose: I bet when I disappeared from lookin' into Lorraine's beautiful eyes, I was gone back to the swamp is where I went, to the swamp, eatin' worms and flies—an' my belly now is full of worms and flies, rotten, makin' me sick.

Tomtom: I got flu bugs up my nose.

Goose: I got worms in my tummy.

(Silence. They are both collapsed, Goose on the floor in the living room, Tomtom at the kitchen sink. Pause.)

Tomtom: It was Bingo. *(Thunder. It starts to rain.)* Bingo stole her gems and jewels. It was Bingo. He was up to somethin'. I saw the sunrise. We knew he was up to somethin'.

Goose: Bingo?

Tomtom: He was up to stealin' our jewels. He was up to stealin' the happiness of Lorraine.

Goose: Bingo!

Tomtom: And his boys. The four of them in their hoods, tyin' me down on the bed, pretendin' they was ghosts and usin' invisible ropes and lyin' to me and lookin' everywhere until they found the gems, until they found our secret things, our secret place, until they took from us our treasure.

Goose: Bingo?

Tomtom: And his boys.

Goose: But we're gonna get 'em back.

Tomtom: He took the jewels because he knows, he knows.

Goose: The bastard.

Tomtom: He knows, Goose.

Goose: I know; I know! But I don't know what, Tomtom!

Tomtom: That Lorraine loves her jewels. He thinks she will follow. It's Lorraine he wants; it's Lorraine he's tryin'

to steal. He's seen her walking on the street, her thin ankles, her beautiful legs. He's seen her squinting in the sunlight, and he must have her. And because he must have
her, he's stolen her jewels in the belief she will follow.

Goose: Bingo.

Tomtom: Bingo. *(Running to the upstage wall, he grabs a
spray can of paint and makes a swirl on the wall, a kind of
notation.)* They tie me up, an' search an' steal, but I think
they're ghosts, an' what could a ghost wanna steal?

Goose: So I come by.

Tomtom: How we doin'?

Goose: Hey!

Tomtom: Hey!

*(Goose enacts the information he is telling, moving about
the room, gesturing and pantomiming in some way the
events he is relating. Tomtom at the wall with his spray can
paints figures on the wall, patterns, concepts, swirls, making notes on the wall, primitive graffiti.)*

Goose: So I come by. You're up. You seen the sunrise.
Bingo's up to somethin', we don't know what. So I don't
feel good; you don't feel good. Bingo's listenin'. I'm pumpin' his sister. We drag her outa her house, screamin',
beggin'; we put the tape on her eyes, we put the gag in
her mouth. I pump her three–four times in the car, comin'
over. She don't know what it is even happenin' to her, but
she loves it. We hang her in the closet. I pump her again.
So I tell you how I was briefly a frog, and as a consequence I sometimes have froglike feelings, so we're both
feelin' awful and Lorraine comes in, she hugs us all, and
then she finds out her gems are gone. *(Tomtom has done
six or seven drawings.)*

Tomtom: I tell you about the ghosts. I promise 'em nothin'.

Goose: I disappear. I'm at the swamp eatin' worms and spiders. There's one spider—he runs on his little web legs—but my tongue sucks him in.

Tomtom: And Lorraine—sweet, beautiful Lorraine, she is so distressed by the loss of her gems, she feels she cannot stay with us guys that she loves, and she is so hurt and angry at the absence of her gems, the disappearance of her jewels, the threat of her own weakness, that she loses control—she loses sight of her love for us, and she sticks pins in our arms, hating herself even as she does it, all because Bingo has stolen her gems, the treasure I was meant to guard. *(He makes a figure.)* So we're talkin'.

Goose: You're talkin'.

Tomtom: I'm talkin'; you're listenin'.

Goose: I'm listenin'; you're talkin'. *(At the door, he grabs up a staple gun and staples the target figure to the wall: staples in the head, the hands.)*

Tomtom: We thought it was ghosts stealin' our secrets, but it was really Bingo stealin' our treasure.

(Behind them Lorraine stands in a nightie in silhouette in the doorway.)

Lorraine: Goose . . . wanna come in here a minute?

Goose: Huh?

Tomtom: How you doin', Lorraine?

Lorraine: I'm fine. How you guys?

Tomtom *(moving to Lorraine)*: Don't you worry no more about anything, Lorraine.

Lorraine: C'mon, Goose; you wanna fuck?

Goose: What? Huh?

Lorraine: You didn't hear me?

Goose: My ears is terrific. So I heard what you was sayin'.

Lorraine: Okay.

Tomtom: He just didn't understand you, Lorraine.

Lorraine: C'mon, Goose, I can't get to sleep; don't you wanna fuck?

Goose: Sure. You know. *(Marching to Bingo's sister, he picks her up and starts for the bedroom.)* I mean, sure, I'll take her in there, you know . . . pump her, you know, whatta I know? She don't know. She sorta remembers, though, huh? So I'll pump her, put her back in the closet—whatever you say, Lorraine.

Lorraine: Not her, Goose; I don't mean her.

Goose: Who you mean, you don't mean her?

Lorraine: C'mon, Goose.

(Picking up the cowboy hat from the floor near the bedroom door, Lorraine puts it on flirtatiously. Goose, putting down Bingo's sister, all but drops her.)

Tomtom: It's okay, Goose.

Lorraine: He don't care; I'll feel better.

Tomtom: I don't care; she'll feel better. *(He crosses to the table for the bourbon, which he drinks.)*

Goose: I don't care; you'll feel better.

Lorraine *(as she goes back into the bedroom)*: That's right.

Goose: Tomtom, I'm scared.

Tomtom: It's okay.

Goose: You don't care.

Tomtom: Just don't make her mad, okay?

Goose: Oh, I won't; shit, no, I won't make her mad. No tellin' what she'll do. See, that's what I don't know—I don't know what she's gonna do and so I'm scared.

Tomtom: It's okay. *(From behind the couch, he lifts a machine gun.)*

Lorraine: Goose! Goosey. . .!

(Goose runs into the bedroom.)

Tomtom: So I'm up all night. I'm thinkin' this and thinkin' that.

Goose *(offstage)*: Tomtom! Tomtom!

Tomtom: So Goose comes by. *(He sets up the machine gun on the arm of the couch, aiming toward the front door.)* Here comes Goose.

(Goose comes running in, his shirt unbuttoned, belt loose. Tomtom throws a belt of machine-gun bullets over his shoulder and pulls a large knife from a hiding place in the couch.)

Goose: Tomtom, she's kissin' me. She's kissin' me.

Lorraine *(offstage, calling sweetly)*: Goose!

Tomtom *(whirling to face Goose, the knife in his hand)*: It's okay; it's okay. *(Goose runs for the bedroom door, as Tomtom grabs up a full-sized target figure and stalks toward the front door.)* Things are getting dangerous around here. Not in any way I can't handle, however, or figure out.

Goose *(appearing in the doorway, his clothing even more disheveled)*: She's got my little penis, Tomtom. She's got it. She's doin' stuff to it. Tomtom!

(Tomtom plunges his knife into the head of the target figure on the door, and Goose ducks from sight.)

Tomtom: It's okay.

Goose *(offstage)*: You there, Tomtom? You there? She's kissing me. *(And then Goose is back in the doorway, just his head and shoulders this time, his clothing even more disheveled.)* I can't see my little penis. I can't see it.

(Pulling the knife from the head of the target, he turns and strides toward Goose. Goose flees.)

Tomtom: It's okay. It's okay.

Goose *(from offstage)*: Is anybody out there? Is anybody out there?

(As Tomtom, using the staple gun, puts another target high up on the wall, there is a loud blast of thunder.)

Tomtom: It's okay; it's okay. *(He moves to the kitchen, pulls out his pistol, and puts the gun barrel against the head of the figure on the door.)* I'm going to tell you a secret. It is night. The fact that Lorraine loves others more than me doesn't matter. It only matters that my love for her is greater than all the loves of all the others. *(He mimes shooting the target in the head and grabs the bourbon bottle.)* It only matters that I . . . stay awake. It only matters that I don't . . . go . . . to sleep. Except I'm tired. I want to go to sleep, and I want to stay awake. *(Slowly, now, his gun aiming at the target and figures, he backs downstage away from them, as if they were an enemy, or the ghosts. He stops very near Lulu, Bingo's sister, on the floor, with his back to her. He drinks.)* But I gotta stay awake . . . because when you're awake, you know what's goin' on, who's who, or if there's ghosts . . . or not.

Lulu: I was born somewhere off in a faraway sky.

(She rises to a kneeling position as she speaks. Tomtom, whirling on her, covers her with the pistol. While she speaks, he relaxes, moves to the table and drinks some of the bourbon. Moving back to her, he puts the pistol to her lips. She is startled, frightened, but she continues to talk. He knocks her over with his knee. He kneels on her, rubbing the barrel of the pistol on her leg and drinking. Continuing to drink and drink more, he sags backward off her and onto the floor near the couch, as she continues her speech.)

Lulu: You were there also, whoever you are. We hung in the air like planets. We fell without falling. I was the child of a person of enormous importance in the high faraway spaces of sky, as were you. I don't know how I got here, nor do you. But this is of no consequence. My thoughts are often the thoughts of someone other than myself, as are yours. But this is of no consequence. We have fallen to this place through an eruption of blood often mistaken for fire. You are not as certain of your royal and cosmically magnificent origins as am I, for I have been here a lesser time than you. All loves that we lose seem the love that we have so long ago lost. But in time, there will be a wind to pass over us, though you do not at this moment believe me, and the awful wisdom of life will be in this passing, and your heart will become the heart of a hero for whom courage is easy, and with wondrous muscles and grace you will arise—armored and declared—so ordained and driven, you will descend upon this place and you will save me. You will be the hero come to save me.

(Tomtom has collapsed onto the floor and lies there staring at her.)

Lulu *(continuing)*: And if you fail in your calling—if you refuse, if you deny me—I will destroy you.

(Instantly Tomtom falls asleep. His head drops. He swoons, breathing deeply.)

Lulu *(continuing)*: It is the law.

(Tomtom sleeps, snoring.)

Lulu *(continuing)*: Can I have a drink of water?

THUNDER AND BLACKOUT

Act Two

Bingo's sister, Lulu, sits on the couch, her hands still tied, the blindfold still on. Tomtom lies on the floor, sleeping in the moonlit dimness near her. Lorraine, in her nightie, comes out of the bedroom and walks up to Lulu.

Lorraine: What's goin' on?

Lulu: Hi.

Lorraine: Hi.

Lulu: I'm havin' a beautiful dream.

Lorraine: Sleepin', huh?

Lulu: Sorta. I don't know.

Lorraine: I just fucked that Goose's brains out.

Lulu: I don't care.

Lorraine: He looked real startled. He was sorta awestruck, I could tell. He sang this little song, like, and then fell asleep.

Lulu: I don't care.

Lorraine *(joining Lulu on the couch)*: You're just sittin' there, all tied up with a blindfold on?

Lulu: Yeh.

Lorraine: Wow.

Lulu: It's okay.

Lorraine: Sure.

Lulu: I am often kidnapped, you know, and left like this to await some transaction both mysterious and grand involving both myself and treasure.

Lorraine: I used to have a treasure.

Lulu: Wow. What kind?

Lorraine: But it was stolen.

Lulu: Wow.

Lorraine: I'm going to rule the world some day.

Lulu: What's your name?

Lorraine: I'm not telling.

Lulu: I love secrets. That's what's nice about being a blindfolded kidnapped princess: everything's a secret.

Lorraine: You're Bingo's sister is who you are.

Lulu: I have my secrets too, you know.

Lorraine: I found you in our goddamned closet.

Lulu: I bet you were surprised.

(Tomtom is stirring. His arms sort of flap, as if he were trying to fly or swim.)

Lorraine: He's moving.

Lulu: What's he doing?

Lorraine: I don't know.

Lulu: I told him a story and he fell asleep.

Lorraine: He's like flying or something.

Lulu: Wow.

Lorraine: We could talk to him. You ever do that thing, you know, where you talk to people when they're sleeping and they'll do whatever you want because they're like under your spell in their sleeping, or if they won't do whatever you want, they'll talk to you about everything? Or if they won't tell you everything, they will at least some things, sort of.

Lulu: I never did that.

Lorraine: Sure. *(She is easing near to Tomtom.)*

Lulu: Wanna?

Lorraine: Be fun. Sure. Tomtom?

Lulu: What's he doing?

Lorraine: Tomtom . . . ?

Tomtom: I don't know.

Lorraine: Yes, you do.

Tomtom: No . . . I . . . don' . . .

Lorraine: Wanna go for a walk?

Tomtom: Okay.

Lorraine: C'mon.

Goose comes out of the bedroom, his clothes partly off and partly on, walking stiff-legged, arms extended before him; Tomtom gets to his feet and begins to walk, stiff-legged; both of them as if sleepwalking.)

Tomtom: Okay. I'm goin' for a walk. And in . . . my walking, there is stuff under my feet to keep my feet from falling right on through the holes to this big big hole. And I don't wanna go there.

Lorraine *(looking at Goose and Tomtom)*: Ohhhhh. . . .

Lulu: What's going on?

Lorraine: They're both so cute.

Tomtom: Giants, bigger than the wind, are all over the place and these very, very old old giants are throwing secrets harder than rocks at Tomtom. Who is going to help Tomtom?

Lorraine: Lorraine.

Tomtom: No.

Lorraine: Sure.

Tomtom: Lorraine loves Goose. I know. What's this? *(He has walked up against a side wall.)*

Lorraine *(whispering)*: What is it?

Tomtom: It's very worrying for me not to know what's going on beyond this thing, and I feel like there's many things zooming and crashing just beyond it and nobody knows what Tomtom is, not even Lorraine. All of 'em thinking I'm this thing inside this other thing on my shoulders—*(His hands are pressing his head.)*—this thing in here like a many-colored cauliflower. I ain't no many-colored cauliflower—I ain't—and if she knew what I was really, she would love me.

Lorraine: What are you really?

Tomtom: I don't know. But I'm very lovable.

Lorraine: No.

Tomtom: I am, I am.

Lorraine: No.

Tomtom: I am.

Lorraine: Come on over here. *(She settles onto the floor, leaning against the hassock.)*

Tomtom: I gotta step real little as a bug so I don't fall through the stuff that is over the hole and into the hole.

Lorraine: What hole?

(He stops and starts back toward the wall again.)

Lorraine *(continuing)*: Tomtom, don't you hear me?

Tomtom: What was this again? *(He is pressing his hand on the wall.)*

Lulu: He sounds so worried.

Tomtom: Oh. I can't get behind it, though. Where's Goose? Is Goose behind it?

(Tomtom smashes his fist into the wall, driving a huge hole into the wall, the noise waking Goose up. He looks about, pulling on his clothes.)

Lorraine: Wow. You sure ain't boring, Tomtom. I hate boring guys, and you sure ain't boring.

Tomtom: 'At's the hole. I went through the hole. I told you it was a dangerous place and holes was here. 'At's a hole.

Goose *(running to look at the hole)*: 'At's a hole.

Tomtom: This is the hole in which Tomtom lives. My name is Tomtom and I live in that hole?

Goose: I was sleeping.

Tomtom: I was sleeping.

(Rubbing his eyes, Goose moves to the kitchen for a cup of old coffee.)

Goose: You doin' okay?

Tomtom: Good. You? *(Tomtom moves to the armchair and the newspaper.)*

Goose: Great. Have a good sleep?

Tomtom: Oh, yeh.

Goose: Me, too.

Lorraine: I slept great. I slept fantastic. I used to think of Goose as a skinny guy, one arm real funny so he couldn't bend it, and this tilt to his shoulders like he was gonna run away. He was short and hump-backed, sorta, these ugly green pimples under his arms. But last night, I says to him last night, "Give me your liver, Goose; hand me your liver," and he did. We were making love, see. *(She takes a wet meaty hunk from the pocket of the robe she has put on as she talked. She squeezes the wet hunk of meat.)*

Goose: Aggggggggghhhhhhhhhh!

Lorraine *(running to Goose)*: I won't do that again; I won't. I won't.

Tomtom: You want my liver, Lorraine. You can have it. *(He is reaching inside his shirt.)*

Lorraine: I have his, Tomtom, so I don't need yours. I mean, in there in the dark, he just got taller and his skin was smooth. I told him of the power he had inside him 'cause I felt it inside me, an' his eyes, I told him, were sweet as the eyes of all the bears and bunnies of the world. Sweet Goose, maned like a dream horse. I mean, you've tried to make me feel that way, haven't you, Tomtom? I mean, I don't quite remember. No. Yes. Wasn't that you, Tomtom? Do you remember? Ohhh, I'm so confused. *(She has ended up near Tomtom. She hugs him.)*

Tomtom *(crossing or turning away from her to his newspaper)*: Yes, I do. I do remember.

Lorraine: Anyway, he pounded away on me and it was like he knew in his stallion's heart more of me than I had thought any man or beast would ever know. My darling Goose.

(She squeezes the liver out of confusion, enthusiasm, and passion. Goose screams.)

Lorraine *(continuing)*: I'm sorry, Goose. I won't do that again. I won't. I won't. I'm just in such a tizzy. *(She runs from the room.)*

Lulu: What's for breakfast?

Tomtom: Where's your cowboy hat?

Goose: I left it. You want me to get it? I can get it. You ain't mad at me? Don't be mad at me.

Tomtom: I ain't mad at you. *(Tomtom changes the bandage on his head.)*

Goose: I feel like you're gonna beat me up. You wanna beat me up?

Tomtom: No.

Goose: I feel like you're gonna—like you're gonna knock me down on the floor and kneel on my shoulders and punch me inna face. I feel like you're gonna do that? Don't. Okay?

Tomtom: I don't wanna.

Goose: It scares me to think you're gonna.

Tomtom: I ain't.

Goose: I got it in my head you wanna. Who's puttin' it in my head you do if you don't? I don't know. You don't know. It's confusin'. You promise you ain't.

Tomtom: I ain't. I ain't. I promise.

Goose: 'Cause I don't feel so good.

(He turns his back and sits down. Tomtom speeds to the pile of chairs in the corner, grabbing one and moving toward Goose.)

Goose: I didn't get much sleep. I got these pins. I got no liver. You know what I mean.

(Tomtom hits him with a chair. It shatters. Goose, yelping, sprawls on the floor.)

Goose *(continuing)*: Ohhhh, shit. What happened? Ohhhh.

Lulu: I think Tomtom hit you with something.

Tomtom: Who asked you? Fuck you!

Goose: What's she talkin' about?

Tomtom: I don't know. Who asked her, anyway?

Goose: She shouldn't even be out here. Who left her out all night? She oughta be in the goddamn closet where she belongs.

(Tomtom hauls her off into the bedroom.)

Goose *(continuing)*: Get her the hell outa here, Tomtom. Goddamn chair, committin' suicide on my head, man.

Come across the room, I guess? You see it? What was the matter with it, was it mad or something?

Tomtom *(returning)*: I was lookin' out the window there.

Goose: Stupid chair. Stupid goddamn chair. So how we doin'? So I come by, right? So we was talkin' about dreams. I come by an' I'm askin' you, you're tellin' me, right?

Tomtom: You askin' me to say to you what I already said to you?

Goose: No.

Tomtom: So whatta you askin' me?

Goose: I don't know.

Tomtom: Go get your hat.

Goose: I don't know where I left it.

Tomtom: I wanna see you with your hat on.

Goose: I'm tryin' to remember.

Tomtom: You said you knew where it was.

Goose: I thought I did. I mean, it's my hat, so I oughta know where it is, an' on accounta I usually do, I thought I did, but I don't. *(He wanders around, looking in drawers, under chairs, the couch.)*

Tomtom: I wanna see you in it; I like to see you in it. You could do anything.

Goose: I wish I knew where it was.

Tomtom: You could do anything, you was in your hat.

Goose: Like what?

Tomtom: Anything! Like anything! Fly or sing. You could fly; you could sing.

Goose: I could fly?

Tomtom: In your hat.

Goose: In my hat.

Tomtom: I'm tellin' you.

Goose: I wish I could find it. I . . .

Tomtom: You could sing.

Goose: If I was doin' it, you could be seein' it. Me in my cowboy hat up high in the air.

Tomtom: And me lookin' up at your singin', and you're pokin' the stars with your fingers. You're flyin' and singin'.

Goose: But what am I singin'?

Tomtom: It's beautiful.

Goose: I'm singin' beautiful? Ohhh, I love you, Tomtom.

Tomtom: I love your beautiful flyin' and singin', Goose.

Goose: I'm happy to be doin' it.

Tomtom: I'm happy to be seein' it.

Goose: I'm happy my doin' it makes you happy, Tomtom, an' I can count on you, right?

Tomtom: Of course you can.

Goose: I can count on you helpin' me be on the lookout for anymore chairs or anything about to jump up and hit me like chairs or tables or lamps or anything. Trees? I can count on you.

Tomtom: Sure.

(Loud knocking at the door. Pause; they look at the door, back at each other. Knocking.)

Tomtom *(continuing)*: You tole me somethin' and I been tryin' to remember—how you was sometimes some other creature—some other kind of creature than a person.

Goose: I tole you?

(Loud knocking.)

Tomtom: Yeh. It seemed of the most importance. *(Tomtom is moving to the door to peep out an eyehole. More loud knocking.)*

Goose: And it seemed of the most importance.

Tomtom: Yeh. But I don't remember. *(He looks at Goose.)* Bingo's at the door.

Goose: Bingo?

Tomtom: Yeh. You was a frog. Frog.

(Loud knocking.)

Goose: Lorraine tole me how you would like me to think I been a frog, Tomtom, but she says I never was. I am him who Lorraine says Tomtom would like him to think of himself as a froggy person, but thanks to her, he ain't. But I don't know what I think. I think I was.

Tomtom: I think you was, too.

(More loud knocking.)

Tomtom *(continuing)*: Bingo's at the door.

Goose: Bingo?

Tomtom: Yeh.

(Loud knocking.)

Tomtom *(continuing)*: He's at the door.

Goose: Bingo, huh?

Tomtom: Yeh. So let's let him in. You wanna?

Goose: I wanna.

(They are taking out their guns. They hide, Tomtom positioning himself so he will be behind the door when it opens.)

Tomtom: I wanna.

(Tomtom reaches, pulls the door so it opens inward. Bingo is there, staring in. Wearily he steps in, looking about, almost sniffing, as he steps further and further into the house. He is neatly dressed in a dark pinstripe suit. They show themselves behind him, both guns against his head, one on either side.)

Tomtom: Bingo, I would come in very softly if I were you, and I would sit in that chair in preparation to being tied up if I were you. *(Tomtom indicates the office chair, which he kicks out from the kitchen table.)*

Bingo: So what's this?

Tomtom: You gonna sit in that chair? *(Both guns are still against Bingo's head.)*

Bingo: Sure. You got a gun on me.

Tomtom: We got some questions to ask you. *(He moves to the piles of crates.)*

Bingo: I didn't expect this.

Goose: You ain't so big, Bingo. You ain't such a big guy.

Bingo: Yeh?

Goose: I thought you was bigger. Wasn't you bigger? You been bigger.

Bingo: I don't know what you are talkin' about. What's he talkin' about?

Goose: What I am talkin' about is you been bigger. Last time I saw you, you was bigger. *(Goose is perhaps trying to measure himself against Bingo, and in this way interfering with getting him into the chair.)*

Bingo: This is my size. This is the size I am.

Goose: No, no. You was bigger. You been bigger.

Bingo: This is as big as I am. This is the size I always been.

Goose: Bingo, fuck you—I got it right here in my memory, and last time I saw you, you was bigger. You was a lot bigger. Or maybe I was littler. *(Tomtom returns with a folder.)* Tomtom, was I littler? *(Having gotten Bingo to the chair, they squabble behind him.)*

Tomtom: Don't worry about it.

Goose: I ain't worried.

Tomtom: You look worried.

Goose: Fuck how I look—it's just these expressions on my face. You gotta be like me and just don't pay no attention to 'em.

Tomtom: Hey! Bingo!

Bingo: Yeh.

Goose: So what's up?

Tomtom: He don't know.

Goose: We got our guns.

Tomtom: I got my gun. *(He pulls out his gun.)*

Goose: He got his gun. *(They are sticking their guns in Bingo's ears, his nose.)* We was talkin' earlier about we should maybe kill somebody if we wanted, an' maybe it could be you. We don't know, however. We don't know if we want to or if we don't or if it could be you.

Tomtom: We got our ideas.

Goose: Oh. Yeh. We got our ideas. I got my ideas. He got his. I got my ideas; I got my shoes. *(Goose veers off into the real objects here, getting lost in them.)* I got my pants. I got my socks, my shirt, my undershirt. He got his pants. I got my socks. He got his shoes. My shirt, my undershirt. I got them. He got his. It's okay.

Tomtom *(sitting back in a chair, Tomtom tosses the ropes to Goose)*: So how come you come by, Bingo?

Goose *(dangling the ropes in front of Bingo)*: You probably thought we would be nice to you, huh? You probably thought we would teach you tricks, give you food.

Bingo: My sister has been stolen.

Goose: Oh, yeh?

Tomtom: Is that right?

Bingo: I don't know what she was exactly, except it is distressin' on accounta how I ain't nothin' without her.

Tomtom: An' how did this happen, Bingo? *(He goes to the wall with the contents of the folder as Goose searches Bingo for weapons and find none.)*

Bingo: I didn't always pay the best attention to her, but I was planning on it. The time was coming. I mean, what's a man without his sister?

Goose: I don't know. That is not a question I can answer. Tomtom could perhaps answer it, but he is busy.

Bingo: I been wandering around ever since. I been holding my hand out like her hand might be in it. It makes me feel better. I was in one room, she was in another.

Goose: It is my understanding you and your sister was quite intimate?

Bingo: She helped me keep my bearings. We was from the same womb, me and her. We come out one after the other. There were of course intervening years.

(Goose begins tying Bingo to the chair, tying his arms to the chair arms and looping the rope around Bingo's chest a number of times. Perhaps in the later part of Bingo's speech, Tomtom makes a few more drawings on the wall, notations. During the interrogation of Bingo, any physical abuse of Bingo by Goose should duplicate precisely what Tomtom did to Goose in Act One.)

Bingo *(continuing)*: I am being punished and I deserve it, but I can't stand it. I expected some other punishment, to be shot or maimed. But not to lose my sister and feel so lost. We was making plans for our future. Certain changes were going to be made. I heard a noise, a sort of half a scream, but I however paid no attention. I was deep in thought and worry, knowing how I did how I was going to be punished. I knew people everywhere was angry at me because I been poor and I been mean, so I done dirt. But

I got a right to my own sister. We would hug. We would pet. I could whirl her by the legs and she would howl. It made me feel good. I know I got reasons for which I can be punished. I blown people away. I'm a action guy, whatas anybody want? I done dynamite and sealed away many a problem and got away clean, 'cause I know who was who from the day I showed up—So I buried many a person out in the marshes so his guts are huggin' the roots a flowers and he's eye to eye with many a dead rat, but I still got a right to see my own sister. I can't live without her. I lied. I lied. There was scarcely any intervening time between my sister's arrival here and my own. We were twins. We were planning a walk in the woods, holding hands. I could look into her face and see my own. And then I came out of that room and she was gone. It was as if a terrible wind had blown through that room and taken her. I called her name. I could hear the wind receding. In the hallway, I found an old woman, a hag of a woman, and she was smoking a pipe and smiling. She looked in the direction my sister had gone, and I followed her glance. I been on the street. I followed a trail of old roses and bits of clothing. Paper bags. Debris arranged in a cryptic manner. I've been alone. I saw your light. I couldn't bear it anymore. I needed human voices. I needed to tell my story. I waited for daybreak. I had a premonition there would be trouble. No one came or went. I waited. I knocked. You let me in. You tied me up.

(Tomtom now grabs Bingo's chair and wheels him up to the wall, where Tomtom points to one of the drawings.)

Tomtom: So, Bingo. This is Goose comin' by. You get it? He come by.

Bingo: Sure.

Tomtom: *(another drawing)*: So here's this dream, you have 'em in the night, you're on your back, you know what I mean—they're a lotta shit.

Bingo: Right. So when was this? *(Tomtom has moved to another drawing.)*

Tomtom: So this is a sort of code drawing here, for something very secret and of the most great significance that happens between Lorraine who you don't know and Goose and me—it is of such significance that I have drawn a secret way of drawing it that only Goose and me can understand. But it changes our lives an' involves pins. *(He indicates another drawing.)* And here is the sunrise when I saw it and Goose didn't. *(Another drawing.)* And Goose is flying here in his hat. *(Another drawing.)* And Goose was some other creature of which we no longer speak. *(Another drawing.)* And Goose was hit by a leaping chair for no reason. *(Another drawing.)* And Lorraine was sad. *(The target figure on the door.)* And here are you stealin' our diamonds and gems. You didn't know we had your number in a picture, huh? Did you?

Bingo: What?

Tomtom: This is you, Bingo, you stealin' the fuckin' diamonds. How about that?

Bingo: Whoa, now.

Tomtom: Sneakin' and stealin'.

Bingo: Whoa, now.

Tomtom *(indicating a drawing)*: Here is you tied to a chair and talkin'. *(Pointing to the real Bingo in the chair.)* And here you is confessin'.

Bingo: Whoa, now. *(Perhaps moving himself away, downstage.)*

Tomtom: Whoa, now, what? You ain't thinkin' you can outmaneuver us when you are tied to a chair.

Bingo: I ain't stolen nothin'.

Tomtom: You are right here confessin' to it!

Bingo: I ain't.

Tomtom: You are! *(He hurries over the drawings again.)* Goose comin' by, an' the dream shit an' the secret and the sun. Goose flyin', Goose was a frog, Lorraine's sad, you stealin', and you confessin'.

Bingo: No.

Goose: You was up to somethin'!

Bingo: I ain't been up to nothin'. I never been up to nothin'. I tole you people was thinkin' I was, but I wasn't. You was the people. I tole you.

Goose: What you was up to was wirin' us, and eavesdroppin' on us, and listenin' in is how you knew!

Bingo: I didn't.

Goose: You jus' said you did. You knew.

Bingo: Knew what?

Goose: People was thinkin' you was up to somethin'.

Bingo: You was.

Goose: That's what I'm sayin'.

Bingo: That's what I'm sayin'.

Goose: I'm sayin' it!

Bingo: But I wasn't.

Goose: I heard you.

Bingo: No.

Goose: We got your number, Bingo! Right, Tomtom?

Tomtom: We got it.

Bingo *(seeing the hole Tomtom punched in the wall)*: What's a hole?

Tomtom: What?

Bingo: What's a hole?

Tomtom: Hi, my name is Tomtom. I live in that hole. That's where I live. That's where we all live. Inna hole. Whatta you think the fuckin' hole is?

Bingo: I didn't know.

Tomtom: I'm tellin' you. *(Lorraine enters wearing a robe, carrying pairs of shoes and stockings.)*

Lorraine: Hi, everybody. Hi.

Goose: Hi, Lorraine.

Tomtom: Hi, Lorraine.

Lorraine: Oh, you got him. Hi, Bingo.

Bingo: Hello, Lorraine. They got me tied to this chair.

Lorraine *(flopping onto the couch)*: I can see that. Goose, would you help me put on my stocking?

Goose: Huh?

Lorraine: You know. Please. And I don't know which shoes to wear—these or these. What do you think?

Goose: Tomtom?

Tomtom: It's okay.

Lorraine: Help me with my stockings first, all right, Goosey? (*Goose kneels before her. Tomtom hurries to the wall, to draw.*)

Tomtom: Here is Goose helping Lorraine with her stockings.

Lorraine: Aren't they nice. Just roll them up my leg. Just slip them on my little foot and roll them. Good Goosey. That's a good Goosey.

Goose: How's my liver?

Lorraine: Fine. It's real fine; I'm takin' good care of it.

Goose: I don't miss it.

Tomtom: You can have my liver if you want it, Lorraine.

Lorraine: I don't.

Tomtom: You can have it if you want it. I mean, you change your mind, you let me know. Or my kidney, pituitary gland. You lemme know.

Lorraine: I don't like these shoes. I just don't like them. Do you, Goose? Neither pair.

Goose: No.

Lorraine: I'm going to be getting dressed and I want your help. I'm just such a little fuzz brain sometimes, I get so mixed up, and I just want to look the way you guys want me to look, so I'm attractive to you—right? And by the time I'm all dressed, you'll have the diamonds, I can put them on as the final touches to my adornment, okay.

Goose: Okay.

Lorraine: I hope you find them. *(She squeezes his liver.)*

Goose: Agggggghhhhh.

Lorraine: Oh, you just look so cute, you look so darling like that, I just can't resist.

Goose: You gotta, Lorraine. You gotta resist.

Lorraine: I know. But you're tough, right?

Goose: I am tough. I am very tough. I am very fuckin' tough. Tomtom and me are very tough. We are both very goddamn tough. That is known. That is not the point. The point is I can't stand you squeezin' my goddamn liver anymore! I CAN'T STAND IT!

Tomtom *(turning away from Goose and drawing on the wall)*: Here is Goose being very rude.

Lorraine: That's right, Goose.

Tomtom: Don't make her mad.

Lorraine: That's right, Goose. Don't make me mad.

(Lorraine storms from the room, giving the liver one final squeeze. Goose screams, falls.)

Goose *(running to Tomtom)*: Where's the goddamn diamonds, Tomtom? We gotta find the diamonds.

Tomtom *(referring to the first drawing)*: So you come by.

Goose *(looking at the drawing)*: I come by.

Tomtom *(another drawing)*: We was gonna rob a bank. You don't know. I don't know.

Goose: The sunrise.

Tomtom: Bingo. The ghosts.

Goose: Bingo?

Tomtom: Bingo! *(He grabs up a chair leg from the floor.)*

Goose: You better talk, Bingo.

Tomtom: You're gonna talk. *(He hits the figure on the door with the chair leg.)*

Goose *(advancing on Bingo)*: Talk.

Bingo: My name is Bingo. I'm not happy at this moment.

Goose *(grabbing up the length of hose Tomtom used on Goose earlier)*: We got ways a makin' people talk, Bingo.

Tomtom: We could make anybody talk.

Goose: Trees!

Tomtom: We could make trees talk, or rocks. *(Goose hits Bingo.)*

Bingo: I started out—I was going to do some big things, gonna make my mark onna world—right onna side a the world—like right onna side a the planet—my name in neon—I knew it.

Goose: So then you come around here, sneakin'!

Bingo: I didn't know what was the rules in this thing a ours from all the days when older guys was making up rules, or I didn't know the way which I could scheme up that I could get ahead, 'cause everybody was keeping everything this big secret. Which I would do too.

Tomtom *(hitting Bingo)*: Not around here!

Goose: Talk, you sonofabitch.

Bingo: An' what I did was scheme up these ways a burglarizing and these other ways to keep no one from knowin' I was despicable.

(As Lorraine comes out of the bedroom carrying a couple of dresses, Tomtom runs to the wall to draw. Lorraine wears the cowboy hat and stops to look at the drawings.)

Tomtom: Here is Bingo and he is despicable.

Goose: And then what happened? *(He has Bingo by the shirtfront.)*

Bingo: I worked very hard. Tryin' to learn the ropes; an' there was a lot of ropes, some of 'em knotted, some of 'em loose.

Lorraine: How's it goin'?

Goose: It's goin' okay.

Tomtom *(indicating a drawing)*: Here he is confessin'. He is confessin' right here, spillin' his guts.

Lorraine: But I mean, Goose, do you like this little peasant smock with the sandalwood flowers, or should I wear the crepeset nylon and maybe a frilly shawl? I mean, what in your opinion would go best with the *(flirtatiously putting the cowboy hat on)* diamonds?

(Goose whirls and whacks Bingo in the head as Lorraine flops down on the couch to watch.)

Bingo: I wanted to aspire only to those things I could accomplish. There was this fella; he was older and he was someone with whom I, for some unknown reason, wanted to be associated and be in his outfit, because he was everything I aspired to. I naturally begun then to follow him. He eyed me suspiciously; on street corners, he turned away. In the hallway to his apartment, he snarled, he spit at me. How could he understand?

Tomtom *(tapping and pointing to a newly drawn figure)*: So this is some guy, you went into partnership with him, am I right so far?

Bingo *(as Goose shoves the chair up by Tomtom)*: I was drawn to him helplessly. I slept by the curb in front of his house and he yelled out the window curses at me. I took this to be a summons done in the strange manner with which a grand creature summons a trivial one.

Lorraine: I mean, I just don't like the crepeset and the smock is ugly. *(She leaps up, hurling the clothing and cowboy hat to the floor, and storms out.)*

Tomtom *(dealing with the figure on the wall)*: Who is this man? What was his name?

Bingo: I don't know. He never told me.

(Goose joins Tomtom up by the drawing.)

Tomtom: I mean, he was the instigator, this guy—he is the party of responsibility in this problem we have here, am I right so far?

Bingo: He opened the door and kicked me. My ribs cracked with a sound that I had no doubt would alter my point of view about certain things forever. I took his kicking of me as a sign I should move nearer.

Tomtom: If we need to discuss this further with this man, where can we reach him?

Bingo: I don't know. He disappeared. I disappeared. I left him.

Goose: I think he's your fence.

(Goose starts hitting Bingo. Perhaps he tries to flee, wheeling himself away.)

Tomtom: I think he was your fucking partner.

Bingo: You're wrong.

Tomtom: You left him and came here. You joined up with your gang in the night and came here in the night and stole our gems after tyin' me up in the night. Do you deny this?

Bingo: I do.

Goose *(kicking something over)*: Where is our goddamn jewels, Bingo? You think you got trouble? We got trouble to make you look like a goddamn happy man at this very moment. You think the air or sun or moon or stars care about any of this? *(Running around looking for something.)* You think the birds or squirrels or snakes or horses or all the other planets care about what we're doin' to you, Bingo? *(He smashes a chair fragment over Bingo's head. The seat of the chair goes over Bingo's head like a collar, and the legs stick up. Bingo moans.)* Those noises—I can hear how you ain't tough in those noises, Bingo. I can hear the beggin' in 'em. And your face—I can see the other face under it—under the tough face, like through the little cracks in the skin, an' it's the truth under there—how you are scared and you are a liar.

(They have ended up downstage in front of the couch. Lorraine comes back in with more clothing.)

Lorraine: Or maybe this swirling brilliant-colored sheer cotton? Or this cotton brocade over satin skirts—and this leather windbreaker when we're out on the street? Oh, you don't like any of them? You don't. I can see it, you don't. *(She squeezes the liver, spins, and leaves.)*

Goose: Agggghhhhhh! *(He falls on the floor. Pulling a bourbon bottle out from the couch, he drinks.)*

Tomtom: Talk!

Bingo: I found a woman. She was dear to me. We hugged and laughed in a big bed. A very big bed. Too big. We yelled across it and sometimes we answered without hearing, yelling at the same time. And sometimes we heard but was unable to yell back, 'cause we was pretending we didn't hear. And there was this guy Joey "the Rabbit"— real name Torretti—and he was agitatin' in this opposition against me.

Goose: This was recently?

Bingo: I ain't sayin', except he ain't on the earth with us anymore, and when the appropriate time should come I will explain not that I am losing any such thing as you might call sleep over it. The woman was dear to me, you see what I'm sayin', but it seemed she was one of those in opposition to me. What could I do?

Tomtom: So you wanted to impress this broad.

Bingo: I take off.

Tomtom: You come here.

Bingo: I start movin' around.

Goose: You come here to steal and impress this broad.

Bingo: No, no. My sister. I'm wanderin'. I run into her. It was a coincidence. Gee, I think to myself, these people I'm dealin' with can do you harm. And then I come out of that room and I don't see her anymore. I don't see the kid no more. And nothing will do but that I must find her.

Tomtom: So you come here.

Bingo: Yes.

Tomtom: And stole our stuff.

Bingo: I come looking for her. Looking for company.

(Tomtom storms away in frustration.)

Goose: And then what happened?

Bingo: You tied me up. I started talking.

Goose: This ain't talking. You ain't talking.

Bingo: It's all I know. It's my life.

Goose: You're tellin' stories!

Bingo: I'm talkin'!

Goose: I'm sayin' it ain't talkin'!

Bingo: I could care what you said.

Goose: Talk! *(He pours the bourbon in Bingo's crotch.)*

Bingo: This is an example of how some people try an' push you!

Goose: You ain't seen nothin' yet. *(He looks around for some additional weapon.)*

Bingo: I'm talking!

Goose: You ain't.

Bingo: Says who?

Goose: Says me! *(He grabs up the gasoline can that Tomtom used in Act One to make his Molotov cocktail and, grabbing newspapers, advances on Bingo, threatening him. Then, as he talks, he spreads newspaper on Bingo, cover-*

ing him, though Bingo squirms and knocks some paper off him, growing more and more agitated.) Goddammit, Bingo! I know tricks! To teach you! I know tricks. To teach you some goddamn manners, you should have some respect for people. I'll do 'em to you like I used to to little cats and puppy dogs and squirrels. Just because you got somebody behind you out there protectin' you, you think you can abuse the whole world. You have been pickin' up some bad habits from somebody. I used to stick pins in their noses. Little puppy dogs. I used to light their fur on fire—little patches—they was furry and I wasn't—people pettin' 'em, huggin' 'em—nobody ever touchin' me. You do me a favor—you tell whoever is behind you, he ain't the only tough guy around! There is us! I used to hang 'em by their little hind legs off high high buildings just to hear their little puppy-dog wail, their little—

Bingo: Shut up!

Goose: You think you're gonna get away with yellin' at me, Bingo?

Bingo: You bastard, who tole you? Who tole you?

Goose: Shut up!

Bingo: YOU BASTARD!

Goose: What's he so upset about?

Bingo *(struggling against the ropes)*: WHO TOLE YOU?

Tomtom: Stop yellin', Bingo.

Bingo: You slimy, slithery bastard.

Tomtom: He knows you was a frog.

Goose: What?

Tomtom: He knows you was a frog.

Bingo (*breaking loose from the ropes and chair*): Who tole you I was a puppy? That's all I wanna know. You slimy slithery bastard, I wanna kill who tole you!

Tomtom: You was a puppy?

Goose (*chasing Bingo with a rolled-up newspaper*): I knew it. Ohh, I knew you wasn't a person. You got those eyes! Ohhh, gonna fix you, Bingo. Gonna keep you inna room. Never let you out. Make you shit on papers, yellin', "No, no!" Ass-sniffer!

Bingo: Nooo.

Goose: Piss licker! Shit sniffer.

Bingo: No-o-o. (*He falls, cowering.*)

Goose (*pounding Bingo and the floor with the rolled-up newspaper as Bingo whines, cowering*): Gonna rub your nose inna shit. Gonna hit you. Make you hide, an' your tail all curled under your belly, your shoulders all hunched.

Bingo: Goose, please. No. No.

Goose: Shit sniffer! Shit eater! Where's our diamonds?

Bingo: I'll show you.

(*Lorraine, dressed as a gypsy and carrying a crystal ball, which seems to lead her, comes out of the bedroom, her manner that of someone who has just been tranquillized.*)

Bingo (*continuing*): I'll tell you; I'll show you.

Lorraine: I'm gonna cast a spell on you; I'm gonna cast a spell on you. And the cast I spell and the spell I cast and the cast I spell and the spell I cast is mud and worms and blood and dirt and "D" and "A" and "E" and "D," only not in that order. *(She settles into the armchair.)*

Goose: Hey, Lorraine.

Tomtom: You got a ball there.

Lorraine: It's nothing.

Tomtom: You got a crystal ball there.

Goose: You got a crystal ball there, Lorraine?

Lorraine: Isn't it lovely? I finally decided how I wanted to dress.

Goose: How you doin', Lorraine?

Lorraine: How'm I doin'? I mean, anybody who can see into the future is doin' all right, wouldn't you say?

Tomtom: You can see into the future, huh?

Goose: I am not surprised. *(Tomtom is drawing on the wall.)*

Tomtom *(as Bingo is crawling toward the couch to sit up, recover)*: And here is Lorraine with a crystal ball seeing into the future.

(In Lorraine's hands the crystal ball moves as if it were a magnet with a changing north. She might end anywhere, and Goose and Tomtom worry that it might be them. She ends with the ball pointing at Bingo.)

Lorraine: And the spell I cast and the cast I spell is "d" and mud and "e" and dirt and "a" and worms and "D" on you, Bingo. *(Bingo has just settled onto the couch, and* *the ball points at him.)* You are dead. You stole our jewels and you are dead, Bingo.

Goose: But he's sittin' there, Tomtom.

Tomtom: Shut up.

Lorraine: Look into the crystal ball.

Tomtom *(drawing on the wall)*: Here is Bingo and he is dead.

Lorraine: It was demons made you do it, huh, Bingo?

Bingo: I had another plan entirely. You know. My own. I was lookin' for my sister; I was plannin' on findin' her.

Lorraine: Not a very good plan that gets you tied to a chair.

Bingo: This wasn't in my plan. Naw. No.

Lorraine: Not a very good plan in which things happen that aren't planned.

Goose: You got trouble with demons, Bingo.

Bingo: No. You know. They talk to me from outa the air sometimes. You know. But it ain't serious.

Goose: Lorraine could maybe help you if you asked, is what I'm sayin'.

Bingo: Lorraine's a cunt.

(Tomtom reaches up behind Bingo to whack him on the head with a chair leg. Goose dashes off upstage by the wall and Bingo falls to the floor. Tomtom clambers over the couch to pounce on him, strangling him.)

Lorraine: It was demons made you say that, Bingo.

(She is on her feet, kicking Bingo, as Goose comes dashing down with the staple gun. While Tomtom holds Bingo, Goose fires staples into his hand.)

Bingo: Jesus. Hey. You guys are serious.

Tomtom: You didn't know that.

Bingo: I want a drink. I gotta make a call. I want a drink.

Tomtom: You ain't makin' no call.

Bingo: No, no. This guy! This guy! Who I let in on my situation and he has certain information pertaining to that which we are all so preoccupied. I gotta talk to him—explain how my current situation is no longer the situation in which I was in when I last spoke with him. You see what I mean.

Goose: You gotta talk to this guy?

Bingo: Yeh. I gotta call him.

Tomtom: So you gotta call this guy—that ain't so hard to see.

Goose: So do it. We got a phone?

Tomtom: We got a phone. *(He shoves the desk chair over to the kitchen table and moves a phone from a cabinet or the desk to the table.)*

Lorraine: He wants a drink; get him a drink.

Goose: I want a drink, too. You want a drink, Tomtom?

Tomtom *(going into the bedroom)*: No.

Lorraine: I do.

Goose *(grabbing the bottle he had been drinking out of)*: I do too. I ain't feelin' so good.

Tomtom (*coming out of the bedroom with a phone on a long extension cord*): Here's a phone. So you're gonna be talkin' on this one; I'm gonna be on this one, you see what I'm sayin', Bingo?

Goose (*pouring a drink for Bingo*): Here's your drink. Here's my drink. I got a headache. You got a headache?

Tomtom: I got a headache.

(*Bingo drinks in one gulp and holds his glass out to Goose.*)

Bingo: This is nice; you gimme another. I love drinkin'.

(*Goose pours as Lorraine moves up beside Bingo.*)

Lorraine: We are going to kill you, you know.

Bingo: I am planning to get out of this.

Lorraine: You and your fucking plans, Bingo. You guys. You fucking guys. You like the outfit I finally decided on, Goose? I picked it for you. (*She twirls for Goose, ending behind Bingo, her empty glass extended for Goose to fill.*)

Goose (*moving to Lorraine to pour her a drink*): It's real nice, Lorraine. How's my liver?

Lorraine: It's real fine, Goose.

Tomtom: Somebody's answerin'.

(*Bingo talks into the phone: Tomtom, up by the drawings, stands with his hand over the mouthpiece of his phone. Tomtom repeats the other side of the conversation simultaneously as would a translator; there is no pause or gap.*)

Bingo: Hey. Hello, Bill, it's me. Bingo.

Tomtom: The guy, Bill, says he's fine, "What's up?"

Bingo: Well, Bill, see, I'm in some trouble here with Lorraine and her guys, Goose and Tomtom.

Tomtom: Bill says, "Yeh? So what?"

Bingo: So I have to bother you about something I know you are going to find distressing. Like you gotta give your share of those jewels back.

Tomtom: Bill says Bingo is stupid.

Bingo: No, I ain't, Bill. C'mon. I'm in some trouble, here.

Tomtom: Bill says, "Bingo, don't you ever come around me with this kinda lame shit about how I gotta be reinstating nothing to nobody I ever ripped off. You hear me, Bingo?" *(Tomtom's manner throughout is the flat, cool manner of an interpreter, a reporter.)*

Bingo: You gotta help me.

Tomtom: Bill is laughing. Ha ha, haha, hahaha. Bill has hung up.

(Tomtom hangs up. Goose whips out his pistol and points it at Bingo's head.)

Bingo: I'm gonna call him back.

Goose: You want another drink, Bingo?

Bingo: Yeh. *(He holds out his glass for Goose to pour a drink.)* This guy, Goose—you know what I mean?—he's dumpin' on me, leavin' me in this bind, here, just 'cause I'm a little messed up—you know—I helped him out; he's dumpin' on me. I been messed up before, he's been messed up, you been messed up—I help him, he helps me, I help you, you help me, you know what I mean. So I'm on the phone here. We're all sittin' around. *(Having* *dialed, he holds out his glass for another drink, which Goose immediately pours.)* Thank you.

Tomtom: The phone is ringing.

Bingo: So what's in the ball there now, Lorraine?

Lorraine: Not telling.

Tomtom: Bill says, "Hello."

Bingo: Hey, Bill.

Tomtom: Bill says he thought he tole Bingo he didn't wanna hear his fucking voice for the rest of the night.

Bingo: We been around, you and me, Bill. These people are threatening to take me out.

Tomtom: Bill says Bingo talks too much an' he wouldn't be in so much trouble if he didn't talk so much around town.

Bingo: So what?

Tomtom: Bill has hung up. *(Tomtom hangs up and turns to start drawing on the wall.)*

Lorraine: I don't know what we gotta do now except kill you.

Bingo: Yeh.

Lorraine *(crossing to the armchair to sit)*: I don't know what else we can do. *(She begins studying the ball for more information.)*

Bingo *(pacing off toward the couch)*: It's a bad fuckin' break. That goddamn Bill. But what else can a wise guy like me expect?

Goose (*following Bingo, his gun out, covering him*): You made a good try there with Bill, though.

Bingo: You think so?

Goose: I'da helped you if I was him.

Bingo (*settling down on the couch*): Yeh? But he's a concrete guy, that Bill. He's got funny tunes goin' on in his head, and he pays very little attention to anybody else's point of view, and that's a iron fact. I shoulda known better, and that's a iron fact. You dance with cement fuckin' guys like Bill, people think you're cement too, and that's an iron fact. You know what I'm sayin'.

Goose: I am listenin' to you. (*He is standing guard.*)

Bingo: So here I am. I'm tied up, Tomtom's drawin', Lorraine's got that there ball there, you're lookin' at me. This is a bad situation. You would help me if you was somebody else—I mean, if you was Bill—but you ain't Bill.

Goose: Bill is Bill.

Bingo: You're Goose. I'm Bingo. Bill was you, he'd be helpin' me—'at's what I'm sayin'. It's a bad situation— Bill is Bill an' he won't help me. If Bill was Goose and Goose was Bill, I'd be okay.

Goose: Goose ain't Bill.

Bingo: No.

Goose: I'm Goose.

Bingo: 'At's what I'm sayin'.

Goose: 'At's what I'm sayin'.

Bingo: We're sayin' the same thing. 'At's what I'm sayin'.

Goose: 'At's nice. We're sayin' the same thing. It's nice we're sayin' the same thing. We're havin' a nice little conversation sayin' the same thing.

Bingo: 'At's what I'm sayin'.

Goose: Tomtom, hey. Me and Bingo's over here havin' a nice conversation sayin' the same thing. You wanna come over an' say the same thing with us?

Tomtom (*drawing*): Here are Goose and Bingo sayin' the same thing.

Goose (*settling down on the couch with Bingo*): So I come by, Bingo. So you come by. So Lorraine come by. So Tomtom was here. We come by; but he wasn't always here, I don't think. He come by. I was onna street. Lorraine come by. I mean sometimes we're here and sometimes we ain't. It's interesting.

Bingo: Like me. I'm here now, but pretty soon I ain't gonna be here. I'm gonna be gone. You'll still be here.

Goose: I'll be here and you'll be gone. Maybe you'll be comin' by again.

Bingo: No. I'll be gone. Do you see me anymore in that crystal ball there, Lorraine?

(Lorraine is doing crossword puzzles.)

Lorraine: No.

Bingo: That's what I thought. So I won't be comin' by. You'll still be comin' by, though, Goose.

Goose: Bingo, if I was you an' you was Bill, would you be helpin' me? (*The gun is lowered; he no longer points it at Bingo.*)

Bingo: No. But if I was Goose and Goose was Bill, I'd be helpin' you. But if I was you I wouldn't be.

Goose: You wouldn't.

Bingo: I mean, you ain't. I mean, if I was you an' you was . . . I mean, lemme think about it.

Goose *(hurrying to Lorraine)*: Take a real good look in that ball there, Lorraine, and see if Bingo is anywhere.

Lorraine: Don't get to be a drag on me, Goose.

Goose: A real good look so your eyes are all squinty an' every nook and cranny has not been ignored.

Tomtom *(drawing)*: Here is the world and Bingo is gone.

Goose: I want him a be.

Lorraine: He is dead.

Goose: You ain't looked everywhere.

Lorraine: You wanna look? Look! *(Handing him the globe, she squeezes his liver.)*

Goose: Ahhhhhhgggggghhh.

Lorraine: Keep looking.

Bingo *(crossing to Goose)*: Lemme see.

Goose: Can Bingo see?

Lorraine: As long as you hurry. *(Together, both holding the ball, looking into it, they make their way back to the couch.)*

Tomtom: Here is Goose and Bingo looking for Bingo.

Goose: I don't see you, Bingo. You see you? *(Together, they sit on the couch, looking into the ball.)*

Bingo: I don't either.

Goose: I don't.

Bingo: I ain't there,Goose; I just ain't.

Goose: Keep looking.

Tomtom: Here is Goose and Bingo continuing to look for Bingo.

(But Bingo has turned away toward Lorraine.)

Bingo: I know you are going to kill me, Lorraine, but how about one last drink?

Lorraine: Make him a last drink, Goose.

Goose: Who's these other guys?

Lorraine: What other guys?

Goose *(moving toward the door to the hall, with the crystal ball)*: These other guys—this whole mob of 'em—real scary guys and they went around a corner—like in our hallway.

(As he passes Lorraine at the table, she grabs the ball from him.)

Bingo: I'm real thirsty, Goose.

Goose: I wanna keep lookin' for you.

Lorraine *(thrusting the bourbon into his hands)*: Make him a last drink, will you? Make him a real stiff one, and then go out and kill him.

Goose: He's my friend.

Lorraine: Make yourself a stiff one too. Make him a stiff one and yourself a stiff one, and then go out and do what the hell I'm tellin' you. *(She hands him the bottle forcefully.)*

Goose: Okay.

Bingo: If I could see my sister, this wouldn't be so bad, you know. I'm ready, sorta. I mean, not exactly ready, but I want her to know I'da stayed around to be with her if I coulda, if things hadn'ta gotten outa control. She's gonna look for me everywhere.

(Goose comes over to Bingo and pours a drink for Bingo.)

Bingo *(continuing)*: Thank you. That's a real stiff one, all right, Goose. Cheers. No hard feelings, Lorraine.

(They toast the air and drink, then hold their glasses out for more. Goose pours.)

Lorraine: No hard feelings, Bingo.

Tomtom *(drawing)*: No hard feelings, Bingo.

Bingo: No hard feelings.

(Lorraine, Bingo, and Goose toast and drink.)

Bingo *(continuing)*: I mean, I know how things work and this is how this particular thing is working here. One more for the trip—one more last drink.

Lorraine: You're a real charmer, Bingo, that's all I gotta say. *(She holds out her glass as Goose pours for Bingo and then her.)*

Bingo: People wanna know how things work, all they gotta do is look around and they'll see things workin' and they'll know then how things work. That's what I done. And there ain't much that ain't clear to me.

(He toasts; all drink except Tomtom, who is still at the wall, drawing.)

Tomtom: Here is Bingo with everything clear to him.

Lorraine: It seems to me it is time you guys quit stallin' and get goin'.

(She marches to the front door and stands beside it. Bingo, rising, starts for the door, Goose with him.)

Bingo: That's what I was thinkin'; was you thinkin' that, Goose?

Goose: I ain't feelin' so good. You got a headache, Bingo?

Tomtom: I got a headache.

Lorraine: You got your gun?

Goose: I got my gun.

Lorraine: You got your knife?

Goose: I got my knife. I got my headache. I got my gun.

Lorraine: You got your lunch? How long you think you'll be gone? I got a lunch all packed; you can have it if you want it. *(She takes the lunch bag from the counter beside her and hands it to Goose.)*

Goose: I don't know.

Bingo: I'll be gone a long time. You won't be gone so long.

Goose: You think we oughta have a lunch?

Bingo: I ain't so hungry, Lorraine.

Goose *(trying to hand the lunch back)*: He ain't so hungry.

Lorraine *(making him keep the lunch bag)*: You gotta have your lunch.

(He takes it and sort of nudges her a step away in order to have a bit of privacy.)

Goose: Lorraine, I was wonderin' if Bingo could maybe say goodbye to his sister like he's wantin' and then he might feel like eatin' an' he'd eat an' my headache might go away.

Lorraine: Sure. You got your plan?

Goose: I figure, I'll be drivin'—he'll jump outa the car all of a sudden, surprising me—he'll run down the road, but I'll run faster and I'll catch him and I'll knock him down and hit him and kick him and shoot him and stab him.

(Bingo's sister, still tied up and dressed the same, still blindfolded, is walking now from the closet.)

Bingo: Lulu!

Lulu: Bingo?

Bingo: Ohhh, Lulu, Lulu, sweet, Lulu, you got those ropes on you.

Lulu: I was kidnapped.

Bingo: I thought you'd run away. I thought you was mad at me. I was so upset.

Lulu: I don't know what happened.

Bingo: They're going to kill me.

Lulu: What? No-o-o. Ohhh, no, don't let them.

Bingo: There's no stoppin' 'em.

Lulu: How come?

Bingo: Their minds are made up.

Tomtom *(drawing)*: Here is Bingo asking how come he is going to die.

Lorraine: Move it or lose it, Goose. *(She flings the door open and marches to the table for a cigarette and her puzzle.)*

Bingo: Goodbye.

Lulu: Goodbye.

Bingo: Goodbye, Lorraine. Goodbye, Tomtom.

Tomtom *(drawing)*: Here is Bingo saying goodbye.

Bingo *(at the door)*: Anybody wanna change their minds about all this, it's okay by me.

Lorraine: No.

Goose: She don't.

Lulu: Goodbye.

(Bingo and Goose go out the door. It is snowing outside. Tomtom follows them a few steps into the hallway, then turns and comes back in, closing the door.)

Tomtom: He was probably lonely, out walking. He thought he'd come by here, have dinner with us. He probably wanted to go out to some very nice restaurant where we could all be comfortable, thinkin' how nice it'd be to share a bottle of wine. A nice year. A medium price. We wouldn't want to be showy. Should it be red or white? One of us would want white. Laughingly, he who wanted white would concede. It was probably his hope that certain antagonisms between us all might be seen to be of no consequence in such a place. Our companionship would have probably consoled him in some way. Three heartbeats beside his own. The steady breathing of four people instead of only one. It would have comforted him. He would have wanted to hold our hands, but he wouldn't have asked.

(Lorraine, working on the crossword puzzle, shifts and puts her feet up on a second chair, making a loud noise. Tomtom turns, draws his pistol, and points it at her. During the rest of his speech, he moves to her, then to the armchair, where he unloads the revolver of all but one bullet. Then, spinning the chamber, he points it at her and pulls the trigger, then points it at himself and pulls the trigger. At her. At himself. Again. Again.)

Tomtom: I could be more beautiful than you. I could. I could make people stop on the street to look at me. I mean, you ain't so special as everybody thinks you are, Lorraine. Just 'cause little people drop out from between your legs sometimes everybody thinks you're special. But I could make people think I'm the source of everything too, like they think you're the source of everything that gets to look into the sunlight and be seen by all the other things that get to look into the sunlight. If only I wasn't so big, so lumpy. I'm all knobby. All thick. But I got a sweeter spirit than you. You ain't so beautiful. But I wanna crawl before how beautiful I think you are. If only I could be so beautiful, I would be on the outside all the sweetness I am on the inside and people lookin' at me would see what I am. But I got potato eyes—boulders is in my bones and in my belly—for my belly— *(His arm is sagging, and he drops the gun to the floor.)* I got—I got—

(The door opens and Goose comes in.)

Goose: So how's everything goin' here? *(Leaving the door open, he carries his lunch and Bingo's jacket and billfold, which he puts on the crates.)*

Lorraine: Where's Bingo?

Goose: What?

Tomtom: Where's Bingo?

Lorraine: Where did you leave Bingo?

Goose: Oh, Bingo. You don't have to worry about Bingo anymore.

Lorraine: What are you saying?

Tomtom: Where did you leave him?

Goose: I left him in a wooded area about five miles from where the murder occurred.

Lorraine: What murder?

Tomtom *(at the wall, drawing)*: Here is Bingo, and he is emerging from the wooded area. He is starting to hitch-hike.

Goose *(sitting down on the couch to eat his lunch)*: I don't think so.

Tomtom *(drawing hurriedly)*: A big truck is stopping to pick him up.

Lorraine: I only meant for you to scare him. To beat him up to teach him a lesson for what he had done to us and the way he had hurt our feelings. What were you thinking to do such a thing? Oh, God; oh, God, poor Bingo.

Tomtom: Don't cry, Lorraine. Don't cry.

Lorraine: You're crying.

Tomtom *(shutting the door, locking all the locks)*: No. No, I feel like I am, but I'm not. I feel like I'm in the bedroom and lying on the floor and crying for some reason I don't know, but I'm not doing it. I'm standing right here. Right? Right? I'm standing right here.

Lorraine: How could this have happened? Poor Bingo.

Tomtom: He had no hard feelings. He was so full of life.

Lorraine: Goose, why did you do it?

Goose: I don't know.

Tomtom: You don't know?

Goose: What are you sayin' to me?

Tomtom: You don't even know what we're saying to you?

Goose: I don't know. I got a headache. I'm gonna eat my lunch. *(They have ganged up on him, and he tries to leave, but they stop him.)*

Lorraine: You can eat at a moment like this? What kind of creature are you?

Tomtom: You slimy filthy bastard!

Goose *(fleeing, leaving them on the couch; he tries to eat his lunch and explain to them at the same time)*: No-o-o-o. No-o-o, I didn't want to. I thought I was supposed to but I didn't want to do it. But I did it. I guess I wasn't supposed to but I wanted to. We was drivin' inna woods an' he jumps outa the car all of a sudden, surprisin' me—he runs down the road an' it's like startlin' to me, an' he seems a whole lot bigger an' bigger an' I got like this adrenaline all in my system an' it's like I was in this very dark room all alone and somebody in the very dark room where I am all alone, yells "BOO!" an' I am almost automatically running faster and faster without thinking until I catch him and knock him down and hit him and kick him. An' that was it, I thought, I was done. An' then this beggin' voice started comin' outa him. An' it was awful 'cause his beggin' was makin' me wanna be beggin' an' what would thatta been but the two of us beggin' an' beggin' out there in the middle a the woods, there's these pine trees an' this snow, an' all this beggin', an' what would thatta been? I hadda stop it. I started it. So all this beggin' was comin' up from his belly and outa his head. So I stopped it at the neck. I got my knife. *(He holds up the knife.)* I got my gun and my ideas. I got my shoes and my socks. I got my lunch. I got my headache. But I use my knife. An' his neck opened up like there'd never been much holdin' it together ever anyway. So I started lookin' around for whatever was holdin' it together ever. An' he started lookin', too. We was both lookin'. I was just sorta wanderin' around, you know, casual. But he was throwin' things—rocks and dirt. He was diggin' in the snow for it and kickin' at the trees for it. He was lookin' much harder than me. I was just kinda lookin' outa curiosity, but he was desperate. He was rollin' around and tearin' at his clothes and I stopped lookin' for it then and watched him look for a while. He looked much harder than me. He looked faster and faster. He looked very hard. But he couldn't find it. And then he stopped, 'cause it was gone, and when he stopped, he was gone and this was all that was left. *(He holds up a little bloodstained sack.)* It come out of him, like on a hiccup, and he like winked.

Lorraine: So whatta you got there?

Goose: It's a little lumpy sack; I don't know.

Lorraine: Can I see?

Goose: Sure. *(He tosses it so that it lands on the floor in front of her. There is a distant rumble of thunder.)*

Lorraine: I knew this was going to happen. I knew it.

Tomtom: You did? I didn't.

Lorraine: It's all bloody. Egggghhhhhhh. *(She drops it on the floor.)*

Tomtom: So what is it?

Lorraine: Look. *(Bending down, she kneels beside it, dumping out the diamonds.)*

Goose: So what is it?

Lorraine: Look.

Tomtom: I'm looking.

Goose: I'm looking.

Lorraine: Look! *(She is lifting the many diamonds.)*

Goose: Pretty.

Tomtom: So whatta we got here from Bingo's belly? Shiny, huh, Goose?·

Goose *(moving to join them)*: Pretty. So whatta we got here, Lorraine?

Lorraine: The diamonds.

Goose: The diamonds? Oh.

Tomtom: These are the diamonds!

Goose: These are the diamonds here, Tomtom.

Tomtom: We got the diamonds!

(Lorraine is putting on a necklace, many rings.)

Goose: We got the diamonds. We was lookin' for 'em.

Tomtom: Pretty.

Goose: Shiny.

Lorraine: Let's divvy 'em up.

(They are taking diamonds too, each putting on a necklace.)

Tomtom: This one's mine.

Lorraine: This one's yours.

Goose: This one's mine.

Tomtom: I like mine. You like mine?

Lorraine: Look at me. *(She is covering herself with rings, necklaces, bracelets, a tiara in her hair. She whirls, shimmering.)*

Tomtom: I wanna put one inna hole. Onna hole. A hole where I live. Where we all live. So we remember it. Hi, my name is Tomtom.

Goose: I like mine. I like mine.

Tomtom *(hastening from drawing to drawing)*: An' one where Goose is flying. I want a shiny one where Goose is flying with his hat on.

Goose: So I come by and these are the diamonds.

Lorraine: They are not a disappointment. Through all my longing, my yearning, my lies.

Tomtom: An' one for Bingo sayin' goodbye.

Goose: Goodbye, Bingo!

Lorraine: I feel dazzling. I feel dazzling. He probably wanted it this way, don't you think? Oh, Goose, I'm so happy.

Goose: What?

Lorraine: He probably wanted to die. That's what I'm saying—it was probably one of those moments. We all have them where we're wishing we might die. You know.

Goose: Uh-uh.

(Behind them Tomtom is attaching diamonds to the various drawings. Occasionally we hear him muttering through Lorraine's conversation with Goose.)

Lorraine: You know the moments I mean. And we probably got him in one of those. He was thinkin', "I don't wanna live anymore. I wish I'd die." And we got him. And now he's in heaven, I'm sure.

Tomtom *(placing a diamond on the wall)*: And one for the sunrise I saw and Goose didn't.

Goose: Heaven?

Lorraine: Of course.

Goose: You sayin' Bingo's in heaven.

Lorraine: Of course.

Goose: Tomtom, Lorraine's sayin' Bingo's in heaven is where he is.

Tomtom *(already busy drawing)*: Here is Bingo in heaven. *(He places a diamond on the drawing.)*

Lorraine: Now that we have at least found them, we must try to make our lives shine with them, our mind to equal their brilliance. Our eyes, we must hope, will flash and gleam, our smiles sparkle and twinkle. We must burn and glow, glisten, be luminous, lustrous, radiant, beamy—

(The door with the figure upon it appears to have moved ten feet into the room. There is a loud rumble of thunder,

the door falls crashing to the floor, and there is a figure, a man, standing there; the walls begin to shake and break open; other figures batter their way through. The thunder roars, and the lights go out.)

Goose: Hey, what's going on here?

Lorraine: Jesus Christ!

Tomtom: What's going on here?

(The walls collapse in several places, toppling in, leaving huge, gaping holes from the floor right to the roof. The figures entering are all in black: long black overcoats, black trousers, hats, gloves, and ski masks. One figure, perhaps, seems to emerge from the floor. They seem to be the target figures come to life. One carries a huge full-length scythe. Others have machine guns. One is huge—ten feet tall—another small, another humpbacked. Each has a flashlight.)

Goose: You broke our walls!

Lorraine: What is this?

Man 2 *(through a megaphone)*: Any movement or further sound will be taken as opposition, and the consequences will be ruinous.

(In the largest, most central hole in the wall, a light builds to a blinding illumination.)

Man 3: DOWN ON YOUR BELLIES!

Man 4: DOWN!

Man 2: DOWN ON YOUR BELLIES ALL OF YOU, YOUR HANDS BEHIND YOUR HEADS!

(As Goose and Lorraine and Tomtom obey, the light in the hole builds and from offstage, through a megaphone, we hear a voice speaking.)

Man 1: We felt this same surprise, this same disbelief.

(In the hole can be seen a man dressed exactly as all the others, ski mask, hat, gloves, overcoat, being borne in the arms of a large man.)

Man 1: We thought our territory inviolable, as you no doubt think yours.

(Borne into the room, the man is placed atop a box, a kind of podium. As he speaks now, the others search. With their flashlights they move about the room. One figure stands guard over Goose and Tomtom and Lorraine, holding his scythe as the others search. One man searches Tomtom while another searches the table, another under the sink, and then they switch, but the pattern is the same: a guard watching while Tomtom is searched, then the table, the sink; and they switch. The guard holds his flashlight to illuminate the face of the speaker. In the holes, once the brilliant light vanishes upon the man's entrance, there seems only darkness. The chairs, the phone, are knocked over in the search.)

Man 1: No one would move us; no one would violate our boundaries. Our big shots would protect us, and we lived by the rules of the old ones such as the "No Hands" rule where no one could use his hands against someone of our own people. We suspected that we were not the center of all territories, but we lived as if we were. We suspected that the earth was round and hung like a cloud in the sky. We made artifacts that were bold and round. They expressed our view of the universe. We understood some things and failed to understand much else. This did not dismay us. The grass was green, and in this we took delight. The sea was as blue as the sky, and in this we saw a uniformity in the design of all things in which our place, should we come ever to understand it, would be equally harmonious. That this time of understanding had not yet come did not dismay us. There were those of us who peed standing up and others who peed squatting. From those of us who squatted to pee, duplicates of ourselves would sometimes drop, squalling and clinging up into the secret place where divinities mingled with entrails and the cord of life ran backward as if through all time to the mystery. This did not dismay us, and we concluded that such mystery was so far beyond our means that we should draw no conclusions but simply express, in jewelry and statues, our awe. And so we lived, delighting in the grass, delighting in the sky, peeing standing up or squatting. And then they came, the barbarians. They went into our middle, and our nation shattered like a great old tree exploding with lightning, and the earth shuddered beneath our feet. We got up and moved in all directions, our people splattering to the north and east and west and south, like vomit from the mouths of fevered gods. So has been our fate from the days of the earthquake and lightning, for all the far places of the world do not know us. Though we could not have before conceived of such deeds, we pillage and we are dismayed. We kidnap that which others value . . .

(All the flashlight beams track suddenly through the dark until they land in unison on Lorraine, who is rising to her knees. Two of the men rush to her.)

Man 1 *(continuing)*: . . . though we ourselves do not often understand this value, and we are dismayed. We struggle to explain ourselves to those we destroy and we are dismayed. As I stand before you, I am dismayed.

(A rope is looped around Lorraine's wrists, and she is dragged off.)

Lorraine: No!

(Man 1 is picked up and carried off.)

Goose: Tomtom!

Man 1: Make no further noises! Mercy is no longer with us. It lies in the dirt of the land of our lost delight. Please, with that knowledge, temper your hatred of us, and live with that fear.

(A huge full moon appears at the lower stage-left hole. The men and Lorraine are gone.)

Goose: I don't feel so good. They took Lorraine.

Tomtom: So you come by. They took Lorraine.

Goose: Are we okay? I wanna be okay. *(The moon, rising slowly, travels across the gap in the wall.)*

Tomtom: Me too. But I don't know. They took her; they took her.

(They are slowly getting from their bellies to their hands and knees. But from here to the end of the play they never again stand on their feet. They crawl from place to place, rise up on their knees to look about; they lie down.)

Goose: Where's Bingo?

Tomtom: What?

(As the moon travels, stars appear in its wake, distant flickering hunks of shimmering rock.)

Goose: Bingo? Where is he?

Tomtom: I don't know.

Goose: We had a conversation. I was mad at him and then I wasn't mad at him and then I was. Is Lorraine in the other room?

Tomtom: I don't know. I'm thinking. No. No.

Goose: We was happy. I was happy, was you happy?

Tomtom: They wanted her. You come by. She come by. They come by. She put the pins. We lost the diamonds, we found the diamonds. Bingo come by.

Goose: It's getting dark.

(The dark is growing. The diamonds glitter all over the floor and on the necks of Goose and Tomtom. Beyond the ragged, shattered walls is a black, black limitless sky spotted with shimmering specks of light.)

Tomtom: Put on the lights.

Goose: Where is the lights?

Tomtom: Put on the lights, Goose.

Goose: Where is the lights?

Tomtom: It's getting dark. Put on the lights.

Goose: Where is the lights. *(He is on his knees, peeping out through the ruined walls into the vast dark.)*

Tomtom: It was them guys. All along, they was the ones up to somethin', an' we thought it was Bingo. It was them. What was they up to? They was up to stealin' Lorraine. Somebody was musclin' their territory—some other mob—so they come here musclin' our territory. You think they was from around here?

Goose: I don't know.

Tomtom: They didn't sound like they was from around here. Some other neighborhood, I would say. That's what I would say. Boy, am I sleepy.

Goose: Now I remember: Bingo gave us the diamonds in commemoration of his dying. I remember. He wanted us to have 'em.

Tomtom: And the pins—the pins we must have in our arms forever.

Goose: I know, I know. But I don't know if I can do that.

Tomtom: We gotta.

Goose: I know, I know, but I don't know if I can.

Tomtom: In memory of her now that she's gone. Ohhh, I'm scared an' I don't know what I'm doin' anymore.

Lulu: I'm thirsty.

Tomtom: What?

Goose: Bingo! Jesus Christ! Holy shit!

Tomtom *(to Goose)*: What?

Lulu: Untie me.

Tomtom: What?

Goose: You says you don't know what you're doin', and I'm thinkin' to myself we should ask Bingo in heaven, an' she says she's thirsty. Bingo went to heaven but he left his sister here. That was him tellin' us what to do. *(He scurries around, crawling, looking for water in the debris. He finds a bottle of water.)*

Tomtom: What?

Goose: Sure.

Tomtom: Ohhhh, I'm so sleepy. Ain't you sleepy?

(Tomtom is preparing his sleeping place, as will Goose. Tomtom gathers pillows, blankets, ornaments from Lorraine, bits of her clothing, souvenirs. Tomtom ends up in his little bed.)

Goose: You know I was thinking what I remember most about Bingo—whatta you remember most? I got a lot of wonderful memories, and what I remembered most is how he had no hard feelings we was gonna kill him. Remember how he said that?

Tomtom: Sure.

Goose: Whatta you remember most? *(He takes a drink of water.)* And his smile? The way he would sorta walk with a little swagger and his eyes squinted when he smiled. I'm gonna try an' walk like that a little and get his smile in my smile. Be nice, an' his walk'll be around, and his smile. Maybe you could do it too.

Tomtom: Sure.

Goose: So we'd be these two Bingos, the two of us, walkin' around smilin'. An' he won't be dead; he ain't ever dead really, if he's walkin' around smilin', right? And if he's never dead and we're him we won't be ever dead either—just two Bingos walkin' around smilin' forever.

Tomtom: Ohhh, I'm so sleepy, Goose, I just can't stay awake another minute. Let's just go to sleep, okay? *(He turns as if to fall into a deep, deep sleep.)*

Goose: Okay . . . except I don't know if I can.

Tomtom: Sure.

Goose: No-o-o, I don't think I can go to sleep, Tomtom. I got all these thoughts.

Tomtom: About what?

Goose: Ohhhh, you know. . . .

Tomtom *(fading)*: No-o-o. What?

Goose *(crawling over to Tomtom)*: Oh . . . you know. Bears. An' other monsters. And furry Bingos mad at me. And Bingos with big angry eyes. And Gooses other than myself, and Tomtoms other than you. *(Tomtom sleeps.)*

Lulu *(speaking quite softly, even lovingly, as Goose slowly makes a nest of newspaper and debris near Tomtom and goes slowly to sleep)*: And of course they will untie me in time—Good Goose and Good Tomtom—for they will in time understand how they must save me, and how, if they do not, I will devastate them beyond what I have already done. They have come and gone and I have waited. There have been bees and butterflies, there have been horses munching grass and snorting in the rain, and I have waited. But they will, in time, see the tenderness of my power, the sweetness of my wrath, and my hands, released, will remove from them their petty little pains, and so healed, they will look at me with an astonished, startled love, a dismayed and hopeless love unlike anything of which they might have ever thought their breathing little hearts to, before this moment, consist.

(As Goose has dozed off, Tomtom has sat slowly up, a man bolting awake but in slow motion.)

Lulu *(continuing)*: And so we will be . . . and be . . . happy ever after. . . !

(Tomtom is staring at Lulu.)

Tomtom: What was all that screamin'? Goose, did you hear all that screamin'? Goose! GOOSE!

Goose: What?

Tomtom: Wake up! WAKE UP!

Goose: What?

Tomtom: Are you awake?

Goose: What're you screamin' about, Tomtom?

Tomtom: I ain't.

Goose: Somebody been screamin'. You sure you ain't been screamin', Tomtom?

Tomtom: No.

Goose: Somebody been screamin'. Musta been her. She musta been screamin'. Somebody been screamin'. *(He is crawling toward her.)* I'm gonna untie her. She been screamin'. I can't sleep with all that screamin'. I'm gonna untie her, Tomtom.

Tomtom: Okay. Somebody been screamin'. *(Sitting, he watches Goose move to untie Lulu.)*

Goose: How's a person ever supposed to rest, all that screamin'? *(Kneeling in front of her, he takes off her blindfold, gives her a drink of water and, shaking his finger in her face, scolds her.)* Now, no more screamin', okay? No more screamin'; we gotta get our rest. *(Turning, he crawls back toward his nest.)* Her eyes is nice. She got nice eyes, Tomtom. *(Lulu takes a drink.)*

Tomtom: Good.

Goose: Tomtom?

Tomtom (*grumpily*): What?

(*The moon is gone now. The stars are multitudinous. Planets, round and ringed, huge and tiny, seem to hover near enough to touch, amid many other cosmic objects.*)

Goose: I know we're so so tired we could sleep for maybe ever, but can you see me inna dark over here?

Tomtom (*looking*): No . . . but I can see your diamond. I can see your diamond in the dark.

(*Goose has his diamond in his hand, as does Tomtom.*)

Goose: Oh, yeh. I can see your diamond too.

Tomtom: I can see your diamond in the dark, Goose.

Goose: I can see your diamond in the dark too, Tomtom.

(*The diamonds seem to have their own light.*)

Tomtom: Good night.

Goose: Good night.

Tomtom: I got my diamond.

Goose: I got my diamond.

(*In the dark the diamonds glow and the night sky shimmers with stars and specks and bursts of light, the actual presence of far-flung planets recognizable and afire, all visible through the ruin of the walls. Lulu sits where she was, unmoving though released, her eyes closed, and Goose and Tomtom lie with their diamonds burning in their hands lying on their chests.*)

The light of the diamonds is the light of the stars, and then more fragments of this light appear on the floor, the walls, everywhere throughout the gigantic dark.)

BLACKOUT